PSYCHOANALYSIS and PSYCHOTHERAPY

36 Systems

ROBERT A. HARPER

A SPECTRUM  BOOK
PRENTICE-HALL, INC.

LIBRARY OF CONGRESS
CATALOG CARD NO.: 59–8169

Current printing (last digit):
17

PRINTED IN THE UNITED STATES OF AMERICA
73220-C

Preface

This book is an attempt to present the main types of psychological treatment in clear, brief, and simple language. Psychotherapeutic theories and techniques included are those which rely primarily on verbal interchanges between an adult or older adolescent patient (or client) and the agent of treatment (variously called a counselor, therapist, psychiatrist, psychoanalyst, or psychologist). Therapies excluded from our consideration are the physiologically oriented (drugs, shock, surgery, etc.) and the adjunctive and non-verbal methods (such as dance, art, occupational, and play therapies).

Readers who rigorously identify themselves with any one of the many systems of psychotherapy will probably be disappointed with the author's treatment of their particular system. There are at least two reasons for such dissatisfaction: (1) Wide and brief coverage of the many systems means that it is possible to hit only the main points and high spots, not the details and refinements, of any one system. And (2) as a non-adherent of any particular system (although finding much of value in many), the author may miss some of the values apparent only to a faithfully practicing therapist of a system. The first deficiency is intrinsic to any broad survey. The second weakness is an inescapable concomitant of an over-all objectivity and is somewhat comparable to the situation where a person holding no systematized religious convictions makes a survey of the various religions: what is lost in fine and mystical detail is more than compensated for by clarity of general perspective.

Whatever the affiliation or non-affiliation of the reader, this book offers a more complete survey of contemporary systems of psychotherapy than has been previously presented in a single volume. Such a presentation should be of particular interest to students of the behavioral and social sciences as well as to the intelligent layman who has heretofore looked in vain for an understandable map of the psychotherapeutic maze.

However this book may be received, the process of writing it has added a great deal to the author's understanding of a very complex and very important aspect of contemporary life. And for this increased understanding, I am grateful.

R. A. H.
Washington, D. C.

Contents

Psychoanalysis and Psychotherapy

CHAPTER 1

Psychotherapy in Modern Society

Psychotherapy as a term, literally means "treatment of the psyche." As we shall see, there are many conceptions of the nature of the psyche and of what constitutes its appropriate treatment. We are interested in the various systems of psychic treatment which depend mainly on verbal interchange, the most important medium of human communication. This does not mean that we shall have no concern about gestures, facial expressions, posture, and other non-verbal transmissions of meaning, but only as parts of systems that are chiefly oriented to verbal interchange.

Verbal treatment of the psyches is generally undertaken only when the patients or their associates consider these psyches in an unsatisfactory condition. Psychotherapy is designed for *disturbed* psyches. What constitutes a state of disturbance so extreme as to warrant psychotherapeutic treatment is also a matter on which varying opinions are available. But, in general, the psychotherapist of any school undertakes to treat the mind and/or emotions of a person after he becomes convinced (by direct observation) that the person is thinking, feeling, or acting in a sufficiently undesirable (or disturbed) way to merit treatment. The therapist must be convinced, furthermore, that the particular type of treatment which he dispenses will be useful in reducing or removing the psychic disturbance of the patient.

Man has known for centuries that verbal communication between or among two or more individuals can have desirable effects on the thinking, feeling, or acting of one or more of the individuals. Both formal and informal education of many types rests on this proposition. Physicians and clergyman have likewise based part of their procedures on this observation. In like manner have politicians, advertisers, and other propagandists. The attempt to induce human beings to behave in what is considered a desirable manner is, in fact, the conscious or unconscious purpose of a very large percentage of human interactions.

Despite the long history of efforts to influence human attitudes and actions through communication, it is legitimate to view psychotherapy, as such, as a very modern phenomenon. Perhaps the clearest point of differentiation between psychotherapy and other forms of attempted behavioral change is the factor of *clear awareness* on the part of both the therapist and the patient that the goal of the whole undertaking is to make the patient's thoughts, feelings, and/or actions more desirable, acceptable, and comfortable to him and his associates. Such clear recognition of the undesirability of existing behavior patterns and clearly stated focus of activity to reduce or remove such undesirability is usually not to be found in other forms of educational or propagandistic endeavors. When education, for example, comes to be an *agreement* between the educator and the student that the goal of the education has become the substitution of desirable patterns of behavior for what has been clearly designated as disturbed thoughts, feelings, or actions of the student, the education has become psychotherapy, the educator has become a therapist, and the student has become a patient.

A certain amount of self-awareness has been achieved by man at other periods in his social history, but never with the extensity and intensity of the contemporary society out of which psychotherapy has emerged as a significant process. The Greeks, after a long period of cosmological speculation, turned their attention to some of the same problems found within the modern disciplines of sociology, psychology, economics, and political science. Then, as now, there were conflicts between old and new values, rapid social changes, and a breakdown of many of the traditional social forms. Social crisis helps focus man's interest on his personal and social being.

Fascinated as we readily become with the activities and utterances of the ancients, we find little among these of direct bearing on the theories and techniques of psychotherapy. Although the Greeks to some degree anticipated modern western man in self-awareness, they never organized specific systems of psychotherapy. Our only historical point here about the Greeks is this: their situation, like our modern one, illustrates the point that *man thinks about himself only when he becomes aware of difficulties about himself.* Thinking is most accurately and simply defined as problem solving. Problems directly related to himself shake man's confidence and threaten his security. Therefore he postpones as long as possible the necessity of facing them. This has been the history of the human race. It likewise tends to be the history of any human individual. When modern man, like the Greeks, could no longer postpone the disagreeable process of examining his problems as a functioning social animal, he began the long journey towards self-awareness. Modern man's look at himself, however, has been longer, deeper, and more systematic than that of any previous human group. He has developed not only scientific observations about himself and his problems, but systematic ways of treating these problems.

It is not our task here to trace the social changes and the scientific discoveries that gradually forced modern western man to become aware of his personal problems and of his need to attempt their solution. First stirrings of understanding that disturbed persons are still human beings and respond to interpersonal relations based on kindness, consideration, and understanding are historically credited to Pinel, who introduced such procedures in the asylums of 18th-century France. Also in the 18th century, Mesmer introduced what may be considered the first specific psychotherapeutic technique by demonstrating the healing effects of hypnosis (which Mesmer mistakenly believed to be "animal magnetism" and which generally came to be called "mesmerism"). But it was not until the latter part of the 19th century that the conscious movement of psychotherapy may be considered to have gotten under way. For all practical purposes, the development of systems of psychotherapy can be dated from the early work of Sigmund Freud. This is in no way intended to belittle some of his forerunners and contemporaries: Charcot, Bernheim, Breuer, Janet, Bleuler, Kraeplin, and others. These men did valuable work (on which Freud in some instances drew) but they were not psychotherapeutic system builders.

Before turning to Freud and his monumental pioneer work, we

shall try to consider in the remainder of this chapter some of the common characteristics of psychotherapy. We thus look at general similarities before considering specific diversities.

In looking for common characteristics among the various systems of psychotherapy, the observer is apt to be reminded of the somewhat facetious syllogism that "all generalizations are false, including this one." There is scarcely a psychotherapeutic theory or technique endorsed today by some reputable therapists which has not been skeptically viewed or seriously questioned by others. Even such a vague generalization as "it is desirable for the therapist to be warm and accepting," will be challenged in some parts of reputable psychotherapeutic literature.

Yet generalizations need not be universally true, to be helpful. As an aid in learning the English language, the generalization that a plural of a word is usually formed by adding "s" serves well. The effectiveness of the generalization is not negated by the ready discovery of exceptions to the rule for forming plurals (datum and data; goose and geese; sheep and sheep; mos and mores).

The beginning student in the survey of systems of psychotherapy should take our presentation of generalizations about psychotherapy in a fashion analogous to rules about the language. In all we say about psychotherapy in the remainder of this chapter the phrase "in general" may be appropriately applied. In later chapters, we shall take cognizance of the many departures from these generalizations.

Psychotherapy begins with a patient who presents himself for help with some problems. He is often partially or totally mistaken about the causes or even the specific nature of his disturbance, but he has been convinced by his own observations or the reports of his associates that he has a difficult situation or set of situations for which he needs professional assistance. This first characteristic of psychotherapy is then a person (the patient) who has at least some awareness of certain neglected or mishandled life problems and a desire to solve them.

A second component of psychotherapy is the presence of a person who has the task of helping the patient. This person—the therapist—perceives that the patient is in some state of incongruence or distress, knows himself to be in a relative state of congruence or lack of distress, and understands the relationship between himself and the patient as one in which he has the skills and knowledge which will probably enable him to help the patient eventually to reach a state of increased congruence and reduced distress.

More than one person may be involved as patient, as therapist, or both. When more than one patient is involved, the situation and process is referred to as *group psychotherapy*. When more than one therapist is working with one or more patients simultaneously, the term *multiple therapy* is employed.

As the therapy proceeds, a third characteristic appears: namely, a positive regard of patient for therapist and of therapist for patient. This does not mean necessarily any deep love by patient for therapist or vice versa. It does not even mean that patient and therapist come to *like* each other (although often they do). But it does mean that they come to respect one another and to feel comfortable and effective in their psychotherapeutic interactions.

Essential for psychotherapy is conviction on the part of the therapist that he understands and empathizes with the patient in his efforts to face and deal more effectively with the problems of his life. The therapist needs to perceive, for example, that this patient is an immature, emotionally dependent, orally fixated, socially ineffectual character who multiplies his difficulties by pursuing his addiction to morphine. But it is also desirable for him to understand with some feeling how a person might reach a point where he could feel so defeated by life (but not to the extent that he over-identifies and becomes involved in the troubles of the patient). He must also appreciate the difficulties of emerging from such a state, and discover ways of overcoming such difficulties from the vantage point of the patient.

It would appear to be also helpful, in psychotherapy, for the patient to have some degree of perception of the positive regard and the empathic understanding which he and his struggles evoke from the therapist. It is an aid to the therapeutic process for the therapist in some way, through words or actions, to communicate to the patient that he, the therapist, does understand and does care significantly about the patient and his efforts to overcome his difficulties.

The foregoing factors may be viewed as generally desirable conditions under which psychotherapy may proceed. Some therapists (notably so-called client-centered ones) would hold that such factors as those we have described are not only essential, but sufficient content of psychotherapy. Most therapists, however, would maintain that with the relationship established between therapist and patient (as implied by the characteristics we have outlined) the essential work of the therapy remains to be done: namely, by various additional procedures (such as those that follow), by which the patient is helped to more effectively handle his problems.

To reach this goal, the therapist provides information and corrects misinformation about the patient's environment. For the patient to make a better adaptation to the realities of his life, he needs to perceive them more accurately. Whether by direct counsel and interpretations or more deviously—through facial expressions, gestures, questions—the therapist provides the patient with a different outlook on his external surroundings.

In related fashion, the therapist helps to alter the patient's opinion of himself. Although there may be outer expressions of superiority, these are defensive reactions for the patient has basically a low judgment of himself. He secretly and mistakenly perceives himself as an unworthy person, and much of the fundamental help he requires from the therapist is in order that he may come to evaluate himself increasingly as a fully worthwhile person.

Another component frequently found in the psychotherapeutic process is what is generally called *catharsis*. The release of pent-up feelings, the revelation of emotional secrets, in the warm and understanding presence of the therapist are generally helpful to the patient. Disappointment, anxiety, and frustration soon reach intolerable levels in many disturbed persons, and the verbal expression of these feelings sometimes helps to dispel them.

One usually desirable factor in psychotherapy is what may be called "home work." The therapist and the patient agree on certain actions (based on the patient's changed conceptions of himself and his environment) with which he is to experiment between one psychotherapeutic session and the next. The patient reports on his successes and failures regarding these attempted changes in his behavior, and then he and the therapist make plans for additional changes. As the patient experiences gratification from successful accomplishments in new modes of behavior, his self-esteem grows. This, in turn, enables him to execute still more improvements in his behavior.

The successful completion of psychotherapy depends on the gradual reduction of the patient's dependence on the therapist. The patient has achieved his improved personal and social adjustments with the assistance of the therapist and has become almost inescapably fond of and addicted to the therapist and the therapeutic sessions. He must be gradually "weaned" from the therapist in much the same way the child is weaned from the parent. The patient is aided in this endeavor directly by discussing his emotional dependency problems and indirectly by his increased feelings of independent achievement. Some of his action tasks between sessions (his home work) are subtly directed by the therapist toward the end of helping the patient to realize his ability to function effectively without the therapist.

So much for the main processes in psychotherapy. Now for the psychotherapist himself. The first generalization about therapists in theory, but not always in practice, is that they are persons *trained* to do the special kind of work which we have outlined thus far. Training in the skills of psychotherapy is generally undertaken by people within the following major professions: medicine, psychology, nursing, education, social work, and the ministry. Although even the theoretical goals of training vary widely for persons in any of these professions who will undertake psychotherapy, it may be generally assumed that these should include thorough knowledge of the history, major experimental findings, and differing bodies of theory in psychology, sociology, psychiatry, social work, and education, as well as in psychotherapy itself. Added to such knowledge concerning normal and pathological behavior in our society (and some comparisons with behavior patterns in other societies) is the very important technical experience of actual clinical work, under supervision, with patients, of thus integrating observation with theory. And a final significant aspect of the training of a psychotherapist is his submission to intensive psychotherapy in order to learn his own deep anxieties, unfulfilled wishes, defense mechanisms, and limitations. Personal therapy is useful in that the therapist learns to use himself more effectively in his work with others.

The *personality characteristics* needed in a person who is going to be a psychotherapist are also very important to consider. Through having experienced intensive psychotherapy himself, the therapist should have been freed of serious emotional problems. But, since the therapist needs to be an empathic person in order to work effectively with his disturbed patients, it seems safe to say that many successful therapists are persons who have *formerly* had disturbance in their own personalities. To appreciate the turmoil the patient feels in his disturbance and the difficulties to be encountered by the patient in his efforts to change (to be, that is, empathic toward the patient), the therapist may profit from having experienced and successfully worked through perhaps not the same, but at least comparable, problems. He must likewise have the intelligence and the superior self-understanding (derived to some extent from his personal therapy) that will enable him to perceive with sensitivity and objectivity the specific nature of the patient's problems and probable routes toward overcoming these problems. If, to objectivity, intelligence, and empathy, we add a high degree of emotional stability and flexibility, we probably have the principal general personality characteristics essential in a psychotherapist.

There are also certain characteristics of the patient which are essential to effective psychotherapy. The patient should be sufficiently intelligent so that he is able, with guidance, to improve his perception of himself and his environment and to carry out programs of improvement arrived at in therapy. He should likewise be capable of rising above his disturbances enough of the time to make possible a fairly consistent use of his intelligence in communication with the psychotherapist. Persons so disturbed that they cannot communicate effectively usually need some other form of therapy (drugs, shock, etc.) prior to psychotherapy. Importantly linked with intelligence and capability to communicate is the patient's realization of his disturbance and his desire to get well. Because of the difficulties encountered in slowly achieving personality change, only a person with fairly consistent motivation to overcome his disturbance is likely to be a successful patient. A relatively intelligent person, capable of fairly rational communication, who is strongly dissatisfied with the present state of his life and is determined to try to improve his condition: this is a person who is most ready to become a patient in psychotherapy.

We have now discussed the processes of psychotherapy, the nature of the therapist, and the characteristics of the patient. What is lacking for us to envision the general nature of psychotherapy? Only the setting and here our generalization can be simple, indeed. One outstanding desirability for one or more therapists to relate with one or more patients in the processes described as psychotherapy is a full degree of privacy. Other factors are also often considered worthwhile. Among such desirabilities would be comfortable chairs, proper ventilation and heat and lighting, undisturbing decorations, possibly a couch, and so on. If, however, the therapist is undisturbed by the absence of one or more such desirabilities, the patient will soon learn to be. Privacy usually cannot be sacrificed, though, because it is essential for the patient to have full assurance that the difficult and delicate matters related to his effort to overcome his disturbances will never fall into the hands of anyone who can use these matters against him.

In summary, psychotherapy is a form of treatment of persons (patients) with disturbed thoughts, feelings, and/or actions, by other persons (therapists) largely through the process of verbal interchange with the specific goal of which they are mutually aware—reducing these disturbances and encouraging more desirable behavior. Here then, in concise form, are the common components of the psychotherapeutic process: (1) one or more persons (patients) with some awareness of neglected or mishandled life problems; (2) one or more persons (therapists) with relative lack of disturbance who perceive the distress of the patients and believe themselves capable of helping the patients to reduce distress; (3) a positive regard of patients for therapists and vice versa; (4) understanding and empathy of therapist for patient; (5) perception by patient of the positive regard for and empathic understanding of him by the therapist; (6) provision by the therapist of more correct information for the patient regarding the realities of his environment; (7) help that the patient may achieve a better self-evaluation; (8) emotional catharsis; (9) a gradually increasing number of tasks for the patient to perform between therapy sessions in applying new information about himself and his environment; and (10) a gradual process whereby the patient learns to become independent of the therapist. The therapist needs to be trained in the behavioral and social sciences in general and in psychotherapeutic activities under competent supervision in particular. He also needs to undergo intensive personal therapy and to be a person with a high measure of such personality characteristics as objectivity, intelligence, empathy, emotional stability, and flexibility. The patient needs to be sufficiently intelligent and undisturbed to communicate with a considerable degree of effectiveness and to be strongly dissatisfied with his present condition and determined to improve it. These elements, brought together in a setting which assures the highly essential privacy and relative comfort, are the substance and basis of the process of psychotherapy.

Selected Readings

Bernstein, Arnold, *On the Nature of Psychotherapy*. New York: Doubleday, 1954.

Cameron, D. Ewen, *General Psychotherapy*. New York: Grune, 1950.

Dollard, John, and Neal D. Miller, *Personality and Psychotherapy*. New York: McGraw, 1950.

Ellis, Albert, *How to Live with a Neurotic*. New York: Crown, 1957.

Fromm-Reichman, Frieda, and J. L. Moreno (Eds), *Progress in Psychotherapy*. New York: Grune, 1956.

Ingham, H. V., and L. R. Love, *The Process of Psychotherapy*. New York: McGraw, 1954.

Masserman, Jules H., and J. L. Moreno (Eds), *Progress in Psychotherapy,* Vol. II. New York: Grune, 1957.

Mowrer, O. H., *Psychotherapy: Theory and Research*. New York: Ronald, 1953.

Seward, Georgene, *Psychotherapy and Culture Conflict*. New York: Ronald, 1956.

Wolberg, Lewis R., *The Technique of Psychotherapy*. New York: Grune, 1954.

CHAPTER 2

Freudian Psychoanalysis: Early Developments

Both from the standpoints of historical primacy and contemporary influence, it is appropriate to begin our survey of systems of psychotherapy with the psychoanalytic theories and techniques of Sigmund Freud. In Chapter 2, we shall consider Freud's pioneer work. In Chapter 3, we'll take up later developments of psychoanalytic theory and practice by both Freud himself and by analysts who remained fundamentally loyal to the major Freudian framework. Chapters 4 and 5 will deal with major departures from Freudian theories or practices by psychoanalysts who are "non-classical," "neo-Freudian," or "non-Freudian" in their orientations.

Although Freud is sometimes credited with having discovered the "unconscious mind," this assertion does not seem to be historically justified. Freud's first psychoanalytic conceptions seemed to have developed primarily out of his work in hypnosis with Charcot and Breuer, especially the latter. Since Freud did not become closely associated with Breuer until about 1885 and since the drafting of their first paper on hysteria was not undertaken until 1892, a number of authors may be considered forerunners of Freud in the matter of discovering the unconscious.

The early opposition to Freud did not stem so much from professional incredulity regarding the *existence* of unconscious mental processes as from shock and distaste regarding what Freud stated to be the *nature* of these processes. Although some writers preceded Freud in pointing out the existence of the unconscious, none, before or since, has exceeded him in the penetrating originality and rich detail with which he described unconscious psychic phenomena. And all these dynamic unconscious activities—the true instinctive molders of human destiny, said Freud—were a kind of boiling reservoir of unfulfilled sex desires from infancy onward. It was this startling description of the unconscious that brought the professional wrath down on Freud's head in the late nineteenth and early twentieth centuries (and, to a lesser extent, on the classical Freudians of today).

Out of first his work in hypnosis and somewhat later his clinical work in free association (to be discussed later) and in his analysis of his own dreams and those of his patients', Freud built his early theories of human behavior. It is not our purpose to give precise historical landmarks in studying this development. In general, however, the psychoanalytic techniques and theories discussed in this chapter will refer to those practiced and held by Freud and his followers from the last decade of the 19th century until the second decade of the 20th century.

As we have said, Freud first began to develop psychoanalytic concepts in his work with Breuer in treating patients who suffered from hysteria. Hysteria (a term no longer employed in standard psychiatric nomenclature) was then considered a kind of catch-all category of highly variable symptoms—sensory, motor, vasomotor, visceral, and mental. For example, paralyzed limbs, deafness, blindness, and other pathological conditions for which no anatomical or physiological causes could be found. With Breuer, Freud found that a patient with hysteria was helped by encouraging her, under hypnosis, to "talk out" the emotional difficulties that apparently arose from early events which she could not previously remember. Breuer and Freud continued this "talking out" process with the patient in the waking state. The psychotherapeutic technique of allowing the patient to talk about his difficulties came to be called *catharsis*.

Both Breuer and Freud soon abandoned catharsis as a major psychotherapeutic method, but for quite different reasons. As far as we can determine Breuer's motives from a not too clear history, he reacted negatively to two developments of the method. First, he found the increasingly obvious sexual content of the early experiences revealed by the patient personally objectionable; and, secondly, he became uncomfortable with the strong attachment patients developed for the physician while the cathartic technique was being used. Freud, however, seemed to have his creative imagination fired by both these facts and used them as important components of the psychoanalytic system that he moved on alone to build. The predominantly sexual nature of the unconscious, as we have already mentioned, became a major tenet in psychoanalytic theory, and strong attachment to the therapist (positive transference) became part of the curative process in the clinical application of psychoanalysis.

Before proceeding with our analysis of the psychoanalytic technique Freud developed out of the cathartic method, we should pause to recognize two fundamental hypotheses in early psychoanalytic theory from which Freud never departed. These two hypotheses, in fact, often served as basic guides in the understanding of more detailed psychic phenomena later studied by Freud and his followers. The first is the concept of psychic determinism or causality, which holds that each psychic event is determined by the ones which preceded it. Mental phenomena, Freud held, are no more capable of existing without causal connection than are physical events in the external world. This is also true of certain thoughts or actions which are usually misinterpreted as being accidental or meaningless. This principle was fundamental in Freud's constant exploration of what other investigators dismissed as trivial, irrelevant, and meaningless psychic activities. These studies, in turn, led to his important discoveries. The second main hypothesis which served as a guide to all later psychoanalytic explorations was Freud's idea that consciousness is the unusual rather than the regular characteristic of mental processes. Unconscious mental processes, Freud found, are of fundamental significance and frequency in human behavior and are usually the causes of human actions (although other apparent "causes" may be consciously ascribed or the event may be written off as a "meaningless accident" as brought out in the first hypothesis). The two hypotheses may be jointly stated as follows: every behavior pattern of man has a cause, and it is most likely that the cause will be unconscious.

By the later years of the 1890's, Freud had reached the conclusion that catharsis in either the hypnotic or waking state was in itself inadequate as a psychotherapeutic technique for exploring the unconscious. He developed his exploratory method of free association, which really became the basic tool of psychoanalysis. Remnants of both the hypnotic and waking cathartic procedures were observable in the psychoanalytic procedure: the patient reclined on a couch; the analyst (in a role of unquestioned authority like the hypnotist) sat behind the head of the patient; and free association itself was a logical extension of catharsis. In free association the patient was directed to let his mental processes go with as little conscious direction (or censorship) as possible and to tell everything which passed through his mind, no matter how trivial, irrelevant, disconnected, or unpleasant. By reducing the filtering role of the conscious mind, the patient was thus more apt to present the analyst with clues which could lead to the unconscious roots of his difficulties.

As Freud proceeded in step by step soundings of the unconscious sources of his patients' symptoms of disturbance, he became more and more impressed with the sexual nature of these sources. Tracing back the roots of disturbances further and further into childhood, Freud formulated the doctrine of infantile sexuality.

This theory contends that the *libido,* or life force, drives the individual in search of pleasure. While this life force is primarily sexual in nature, it includes all feelings which motivate a person to desire pleasurable contact with others or even with himself. From infancy, Freud hypothesized, the individual is pushed by the libido toward the achievement of mature sexuality. If he meets with no serious obstacles, the individual progresses through certain stages of sexuality. If consistently frustrated, the individual may "fixate" his libido at any of these stages prior to maturity and develop corresponding pathological conditions.

The first stage of sexuality, characteristic of the first year of the child's life, is the *oral* stage. During this phase the libidinal energy of the child is centered in the mouth and gratification is derived through this channel. The second is the *anal* stage, at which time the libido partially transfers itself to the anal zone, and intense pleasures are derived from the retention and expulsion of feces. The child's interests during this period (ages one to three) are largely concentrated on himself (narcissism), and satisfactions are derived chiefly from his own body (auto-erotism). His interpersonal relationships are primitive and directed toward partial objects (for example, the breast rather than the mother as a whole). At about the age of three, the penis (clitoris in the female) becomes the focus of libidinal energy, and this ushers in the last pregenital phase, the *phallic* stage. At first in the phallic stage, interest in the penis (or clitoris) is auto-erotic, but soon sexual interest in the parents develops, and the Oedipus period begins.

The *Oedipus* period (usually thought of as extending from ages three to seven and part of the phallic stage) takes its name from the Greek legend of Oedipus, who unknowingly killed his father and married his mother. Freud pointed out that the child in the Oedipal period of life becomes sexually interested in the parent of the opposite sex and develops a feeling of rivalry toward and a wish to displace the parent of the same sex. Soon learning that such sexual interest in the parent of the other sex is forbidden and feeling hate as well as love for the parent of the same sex, the child develops strong feelings of anxiety and guilt. Expecting punishment for his "criminal" desires, the male child fantasies becoming castrated. A comparable fantasy of genital injury apparently takes hold of the female child. Also because the girl observes that she has a very small "penis," the clitoris, she develops a basic sense of inferiority (penis envy).

The intensity of fear becomes so unendurable in the child that he or she is forced to yield to the powerful rival (the parent of the same sex) by renouncing and repressing sexual feelings toward the love-object (the parent of the other sex). This struggle, called the Oedipus complex, was to Freud the crucial factor in the development of personality. With successful repression and resolution of the conflict, a relatively healthy personality develops. With lack of successful working through of the conflict, serious personality disturbances evolve.

Following upon the Oedipal period (and still within the third and last pregenital stage, the phallic) is the phase of life which Freud designated as the latency period. This period of relative sexual quiescence in the individual begins at about age seven and lasts until the onset of puberty (somewhere around twelve to fourteen years of age). The increased activity of the genital glands at puberty brings a correspondingly heightened libido, which reactivates the old Oedipal interests. If a relatively successful resolution of the earlier Oedipal crisis was achieved, however, the individual transfers his or her sexual interest to persons of the other sex outside the family and goes on to mature sexual fulfillment. The libido thus finally reaches its original goal, the genital stage of development.

We'll return a little later to a consideration of some of the psychopathological conditions which, according to Freud, result from difficulties in resolving the Oedipal conflict. Several other contributions he made to the understanding of unconscious sexuality in normal, as well as abnormal, personality development should be given our attention now. First is his hypothesis of bisexuality of human beings: no male is devoid of some strong wishes of a feminine nature, and no female is without some underlying masculine tendencies. Such homosexual inclinations are very strongly repudiated by most people at the conscious level. Unconsciously, however, bisexuality (and guilt and anxiety regarding it) is of great importance in understanding human behavior.

A second important hypothesis of Freud's regarding human sexuality is the bipolarity of human emotions, a process which has come to carry the name, *ambivalence*. Feelings of a positive nature toward a person or group are, according to Freud's clinical investigations, almost invariably accompanied by feelings of a negative nature. One side of the emotional reaction, often the negative, is usually repressed from consciousness, however, so that the individual is generally aware of only one aspect of his emotional response. The parent, for example, is conscious of loving his child, but is often unconscious of an accompanying hostility toward this same child. Such hostility is nevertheless significantly influencing the parent's interactions with the child and is not infrequently observable to an outside observer. The same is true of the child's feelings toward the parent, of the man's or woman's attitudes toward the mate: conscious love is often mixed with unconscious hate. Ambivalence of other feelings also often occurs—happiness with an underlying melancholy; pleasure with displeasure; joy with anger.

Freud's analysis of human sexuality led to a third significant hypothesis which he called *sublimation*. This theory holds that a certain amount of libido which is originally devoted to a sexual focus may be directed into ostensibly non-sexual channels from which either an esthetic or utilitarian pleasure is derived. Stated differently, sublimation is the unconscious gratification of a sexual desire by a substitute activity which conforms to personal and social definitions of acceptability (in the form of art and/or utility). Out of sublimation, according to this Freudian hypothesis, grew the whole superstructure of human civilization.

The fourth important hypothesis which Freud developed from his clinical observations of human sexuality is what he termed *displacement*. This process, first discovered by Freud in his analysis of dreams, is the representation of a part by the whole, or vice versa. That is, when one idea or image is substituted by another which is emotionally (not necessarily logically) associated with it, displacement has occurred. If, for example, a person has had a very unpleasant experience with a man who happened to have a beard, he may displace his hostility toward this person to all men with beards. A part of one unpleasant experience has come to symbolize the whole, and, illogically and irrelevantly (except in an emotional sense), the presentation of the stimulus (any man's beard) will bring forth the emotional response of hostility.

Displacement functions in a number of important ways in psychoanalytic theory and practice. One is in Freudian dream interpretation, a subject to which we'll soon turn our attention, and another is *transference*. You will recall that we mentioned earlier that one of the reasons Breuer apparently dissociated himself from collaboration with Freud in the treatment of hysteria by the cathartic method was his distaste for the strong attachments patients developed for the therapist in the course of the treatment. Freud, on the other hand, was not only undismayed by this fact, but went on to use his observations about these attachments as one of the corner stones of the evolving psychoanalytic practice. This attachment of patient for analyst was actually a form of displacement. The phrase *object displacement* was used by Freud when a love or hatred for a certain individual was denied consciously by the patient and (though the source of the feeling remains in the unconscious) referred to another person as stimulus "by proxy" for the emotional response. When the psychotherapist becomes the "proxy," that is, when a patient displaces to the analyst in the present, love or hatred unconsciously attached to a significant person (often a parent) in his past, *transference* has occurred. Freud found that the patient, in the course of free association, inevitably displaced many important positive and negative feelings.

When transference became particularly intense, the patient would reproduce and re-enact important childhood conflicts and fears.

The emotional experience of recalling unresolved childhood problems (through free association) and facing them in the transference situation with the understanding and accepting substitute parent (the analyst) may be considered the "dynamic axis" of the curative process in Freudian psychoanalysis. The individual as a child was too weak and too inexperienced to solve these problems, so he pushed them out of consciousness (repressed them). Now helped to be stronger and wiser by both maturity and the analyst, the patient is better able to face these conflicts and to gain the knowledge to solve them.

We spoke earlier of free association as *the* psychoanalytic technique. What we have just said about the importance of transference in no way contradicts this. Through the passive, permissive atmosphere of the psychoanalytic situation, in which the patient is constantly encouraged to say whatever comes to mind, transference is likely to develop. Lying on the couch where he cannot even see the face of the analyst, coming frequently (generally five times a week) into this submission-inducing setting, and being kept quite ignorant of reality factors about the analyst, the patient is further stimulated to call forth strong feelings from the past and to attach them to this almost phantom figure of the analyst. Free association and the psychoanalytic setting are well designed, then, to encourage transference. Psychoanalysis, employing the technique of free association, may be considered *transference analysis.*

So long as the patient continues to associate freely, the psychoanalyst keeps quiet. When strong resistances to free association develop, the analyst will interfere only to the point of helping the patient to overcome the resistance and to start talking again. One important aid to free association that Freud discovered early in his investigations derived from dreams. Freud found that many patients, in the course of freely associating, mentioned their dreams and that, when they were then encouraged to associate on the dream material, much new unconscious feeling was revealed. When associations to other topics broke down, associations to old or new dreams often brought an important "break through." Dream analysis, then, became an important extension of, not substitution for, the technique of free association.

In studying the free associations of his patients (and of himself) on dreams, Freud discovered that certain types of displacements were very common: that is, certain images in dreams very frequently stood for or symbolized objects and desires of the real world. These common symbols of dreams generally referred to the intense interests of childhood: members of the immediate family, body parts (especially sexual ones), bodily functions and experiences (urination, defecation, copulation, eating, anger, weeping, etc.), birth, death, and so on. Some of the more common examples of Freudian symbols in dreams occur quite often: money stands for feces, a journey or absence for death, a king or governor or other authority figure for father, a pair of sisters for breasts, a tree, steeple, necktie, sword, snake, etc., for a penis, a box, ravine, book, purse, etc., for a vagina.

Although Freud felt certain symbols commonly occurred in dreams and were sometimes an aid to the analyst in understanding a patient's dream does not mean that such authoritative dream interpretation was substituted for free association. Freud specifically warned against dream interpretation which was not based on specific knowledge of a particular patient's unconscious conflicts (derived through free association). Such knowledge of common symbols would, however, occasionally help the patient and analyst over an obstacle to understanding (a resistance) of the particular patient's unconscious.

The essential assertion about the unconscious mind which Freud made on the basis of his analysis of dreams was that a dream was *always* a wish fulfillment. By analyzing the highly disguised dream product (the manifest content) for its underlying meanings (the latent content), the precise nature of the patient's deep-seated desires can be understood. Freud felt that the study of dreams led not only to an understanding of general unconscious material ("the royal road to the unconscious"), but especially the repressed desires that (because unfulfilled other than in dreams) were creating the major disturbances in the patient's mental life.

Two other aids to the understanding of unconscious motives of the individual which Freud discovered early in his investigations should be mentioned here. These are the analysis of parapraxes and wit. The former are slips of the tongue and pen and memory and many of the daily mishaps that we call "accidents." Such, Freud ably demonstrated, are not meaningless errors, but revelatory of unconscious desires. The man who forgets a present for his wife on an anniversary or who forgets to introduce her at a social gathering, for example, is not just "absent-minded" or "careless": he is expressing underlying feelings of hostility. The politician who says: "Ladies and gentlemen, a vote for me is a vote against honesty—I mean, ha, ha—a vote against *dis*honesty in government" may be revealing some of his underlying motives and deserves to be watched.

In much the same way, wit and humor offer the individual a way of releasing part of his pent-up energy attached to repressed wishes. These wishes are invariably of a sexual or hostile nature, Freud discovered—wishes which, in a serious and open way, the individual could not express without meeting with disapproval from self and others. An examination of the jokes of any social circle will well bear out Freud's observations: hostility, lust, or desires which combine the two are being fulfilled.

Freud's first description of the mind presented it as analogous to a telescope made up of various psychic components arranged consecutively and stretching from the perceptual system at one end to the motor system at the other, with the various memory and association systems in between. This conception was described in his book on dreams (see "Selected Readings" at the end of this chapter for the best English translation of this, generally considered the greatest of Freud's works), which first appeared in 1900, but was never further elaborated. As described in that book, however, the *wish* is the sole motive force of the whole psychic apparatus. A wish was described by Freud as "a current in the apparatus" (apparently conceived of as a psychic excitation analogous to a nerve impulse) which derived from a tension (unpleasure) and arriving at gratification (pleasure) —that is, the release of tension.

Freud's early view of the mind also included his important formulation of two fundamentally different kinds of mental processes, which he labeled *primary* and *secondary*. The primary process is characteristic of children, of highly disturbed persons, and of the unconscious minds of all people. A wish, by the route of the primary process, seeks *immediate gratification.* It is uninhibited by any reality factors, any logical contradictions, any causal associations, any sense of appropriateness. The goal of a wish via the primary process is to discharge the excitation through any motor exit. If that fails, the primary process will find an unconscious sensory route (notably through dreams in healthy individuals and through hallucinations in pathological persons) via the remembered perception of a previous satisfaction.

In the secondary process, the emphasis is on the ability of the individual to delay the fulfillment of the wish. The more mature and experienced person is able to recognize environmental circumstances which are favorable or unfavorable to discharge of psychic energy rather than discharging regardless of appropriateness and other reality factors (as is the case with the primary process). Psychic energy also becomes much more firmly fixed to certain objects and channels of discharge in the secondary process as distinguished from the ready switch of a wish from one to another object and channel in the primary process.

Secondary process thinking is the mode of conscious thinking we usually attribute to the relatively normal and mature adult. It is largely verbal in nature and follows the rules of syntax and logic.

Primary process thinking is the dominant mode of thinking for the young child and persists in the unconscious in adult life and manifests itself chiefly through dreams, humor, pathology, and a few other ways. It is characterized by the absence of negatives, conditionals, or other qualifications; the replacement of an idea by its opposite; visual or sense impressions often in the place of words; and absence of a sense of or concern with time.

As Freud pointed out, it is essential for the psychotherapist to understand the difference between the secondary process of thinking, with which we are so familiar through introspection of our adult conscious minds, and the primary process, predominantly the activity of the unconscious. Without a realization of the quite different nature of the primary process, the various normal and pathological manifestations of the patient's unconscious remain a mystery to the therapist. Light cast on the unconscious and its operation via the primary process is sometimes considered the most profound contribution Freud made to understanding human behavior and helping the individual to overcome unconsciously rooted disturbances.

With this brief summary of the early Freudian conceptions of how the human psyche is constructed and how it functions and of the major psychoanalytic treatment procedures, we need to try to understand a little more specifically how Freud applied his hypotheses to particular types of emotional disturbances.

When, earlier in the chapter, we talked of the libidinal development of the individual, we described the three pregenital stages through which passage is made on the way to the goal of genital maturity. If, as a result of traumatic experiences, a considerable amount of libido becomes fixated at one or more of these pregenital zones, the individual's development toward maturity will be blocked, Freud contended, and some form of psychoneurosis will occur. Pathological symptoms may not appear until later in life, at which time, under the influence of emotional strain, great quantities of libido will pour back into the points of fixation (oral, anal, or phallic). This is the process of *regression.* It is seen in mild form, for example, in a child of three or four, who, under some such emotional stress as the arrival of a baby brother or sister, will regress to the oral stage of thumb-sucking. An adult example of pathological regression to the oral stage would be a chronic alcoholic. The hysteric patient, according to Freud, represented regression to the phallic stage, and the obsessive-compulsive neurotic is the classical example of anal libidinal fixation.

In terms of these early theoretical formulations, the task of psychoanalytic treatment as conceived by Freud was to release the libido fixated at pregenital points and help the disturbed person to avail himself of this neurotically wasted energy for practical life problems. As a result of successful analysis, the libido was set free to follow its course toward its instinctive goal of genital maturity.

Freud made some distinctions between what he called *actual* neuroses and *psycho*neuroses, but he did little to follow up these differences. He devoted his major clinical interest from 1900 onward to what he called the psychoneuroses (hysteria and the obsessions). One type of patient in the actual neuroses was the neurasthenic, a term Freud limited to persons with such symptoms as fatigue, listlessness, flatulence, constipation, headache, and dyspepsia. He hypothesized that neurasthenia developed from excessive masturbation or nocturnal emissions. The other type of actual neurosis, according to Freud, was anxiety neurosis, a condition which he proposed developed from habitual sexual activity without adequate outlet (lovemaking without orgasm or with inadequate orgasm, as in coitus interruptus). It is now thought by many psychoanalysts that these were mistaken conceptions, and little reference is found to Freud's notion of actual neuroses in recent psychoanalytic literature.

Quite the contrary is true, however, regarding Freud's conceptions of the psychoneuroses. These ideas underwent a steady expansion and revision by Freud and his followers well into the third decade of the 20th century. We shall here consider some of the earlier developments in Freud's beliefs about the psychoneuroses.

As a result of his work with Breuer, the reader will recall, Freud concluded that hysterical symptoms were caused by a forgotten event whose accompanying emotional energy had never been discharged. He soon added to this idea that for any emotional experience to be the source of a psychic disturbance it had to be strongly distasteful to the individual's conscious self. Freud thought this applied not only for cases of hysteria, but also for obsessions and many of the phobias. Since many of these repugnant experiences reported by patients in free association seemed concerned with sex and childhood, Freud proposed the hypothesis that these emotional disturbances were the result of sexual seduction in childhood by an adult or an older child.

This latter hypothesis soon had to be altered by Freud. He came to realize that many of the stories which his patients told him of having been sexually seduced as children were, in fact, fantasies rather than memories. At first discouraged, Freud soon proceeded to develop the theory of infantile sexuality, which we have already discussed.

The evidence that patients were preoccupied with sexual fantasies from early childhood onward through life led Freud to place less emphasis on particular traumatic events as the causation of the psychoneuroses. In a new theory which was formulated about 1905, Freud placed new stress on the importance of the patient's sexual constitution and heredity as sources of psychoneuroses. He did not, however, make such sources exclusively responsible. He believed that constitutional and experiential factors both contributed to the development of psychoneurotic conditions, and that either one in some instances can be predominant.

Further revisions of the Freudian theories of the mental disorders (and of the nature of the psychic apparatus in which these disorders occur) take us into the second decade of the 20th century and beyond. We have reserved discussion of this material for Chapter 3.

Summary

From his work in hypnosis with Breuer, Freud developed the method of mental catharsis. This was a technique whereby the patient "talked out" the nature and sources of his problems and thus (in some instances) overcame his emotional disturbances. Becoming dissatisfied with catharsis as a method, Freud extended the technique into what he called free association. In this procedure, the patient, reclining on a couch, tells the therapist all that passes through his mind. Such uncensored recounting helps the analyst to discover important unconscious sources of the patient's problems.

Freud held to the fundamental hypotheses that all psychic events have causes and that most such causes derive from the unconscious. The sources of mental disturbances, Freud contended, were primarily sexual in nature. In his sexual development the individual passes through four stages: the oral, anal, phallic, and genital. Fixation of too much of the libido (psychic energy, life force) of the individual at any of the pregenital stages brings corresponding pathological psychic conditions. The time of greatest disturbance falls in the Oedipal period (within the phallic stage). At this time the individual struggles with lust for one parent and jealous conflict with the other. Successful resolution of the Oedipal conflict is a prerequisite to normal adulthood (the genital stage).

Other important concepts in the Freudian theory of sexuality include the latency period, bisexuality, ambivalence, sublimation, and displacement (a special form of which is transference). Analysis of the transference relationship, by the process of free association, may be considered the "dynamic axis" of the curative process in psychoanalysis.

Dreams and their interpretation developed as an important aid to the free association process in analysis. Two other such aids were Freud's analysis of everyday slips, which he felt were always unconsciously meaningful, and wit, as revealing of unconscious hostility and sexual desire.

Two different types of processes are at work in the psychic apparatus of the individual, according to Freud: the primary and the secondary. The former is characteristic of the mental life of children, of disturbed persons, and of the universal unconscious. The latter is the usual conscious thinking of an undisturbed adult.

Freud's early applications of his theory to pathological conditions stressed the importance of libidinal fixation and regression. He also developed more detailed hypotheses regarding what he termed the actual neuroses and the psychoneuroses.

Selected Readings

Brenner, Charles, *An Elementary Textbook of Psychoanalysis*. New York: Int. Univs., 1955.

Breuer, Josef, and Sigmund Freud, *Studies on Hysteria* (translated by James Strachey). New York: Basic Books, 1957.

Freud, Sigmund, *The Basic Writings of Sigmund Freud* (translated by A. A. Brill). New York: Modern Library, 1938.

———, *The Interpretation of Dreams* (translated by James Strachey). New York: Basic Books, 1956.

Jones, Ernest, *The Life and Work of Sigmund Freud*, Vol. I. New York: Basic Books, 1953.

CHAPTER 3

Freudian Psychoanalysis: Later Additions and Modifications

As already indicated in Chapter 2, Freud did not view his teachings as complete and final, and throughout his lifetime he continued to modify and supplement them. He frankly acknowledged that he was not always certain himself about the relationships between some of his older and newer concepts. He felt strongly, however, that a desire for consistency should not prevent the recording of insights that an existing system did not readily accommodate. While such flexibility is admirable, the resulting inconsistencies make our understanding of Freudian theory considerably more difficult. At times, in an effort to make certain concepts clear and understandable, we may be guilty of oversimplification.

The first Freudian conception of the human mind as analogous to an optical instrument (presented in 1900 in *The Interpretation of Dreams*) was never, as we mentioned in Chapter 2, further elaborated. In 1913, however, Freud made a new effort to develop a topography of the mind by dividing its contents and operations into three mental systems: Ucs. (unconscious), Pcs. (preconscious), and Cs. (conscious). This differentiation between preconscious and unconscious mental activities is important in psychoanalysis. Thoughts on which awareness is not currently centered (hence, not immediately conscious), but which are recallable by an effort of the will constitute

Pcs., the preconscious. The group of mental processes and contents which make up Ucs., the unconscious, are at least temporarily barred from access to consciousness by some force within the mind itself and cannot be reached by an effort of attention on the part of the individual.

In 1923, Freud proposed a third and final general hypothesis concerning mental systems. This third theory is called the structural hypothesis to distinguish it from the topographic theory just mentioned. In this latest conception, Freud distinguished three functionally related structures of the mind: the id, the ego, and the superego. In general, the id represents the basic drives (instincts), the ego is the mediator between the id and external reality, and the superego comprises the individual's moral precepts and ideal aspirations (roughly, his conscience).

By the time he developed the structural hypothesis, Freud had somewhat changed his point of view regarding the instinctual nature of man. The reader will remember from the preceding chapter that for a long time Freud considered all instinctual manifestations of the individual a part of the sexual drive. Around 1920, however, mainly as a result of his study of masochism and sadism (the former is the pathological enjoyment of receiving pain and the latter of seeing others suffer), he proposed the existence of another basic drive in addition to the sexual: the aggressive drive or "death instinct." He considered the two drives fused in both normal and pathological activities, but in varying amounts and intensities. The term "Eros" (life) was employed to refer to the sexual drive, and the term "Thanatos" (death) to refer to the aggressive drive.

Freud believed that the aggressive drive showed the same capacity for fixation and regression and the same development through the oral, anal, phallic, and genital phases as the sexual drive. The relationship of the aggressive drive and various parts of the body is not so close as for sex, but it is still apparent. Biting, for example, is a characteristic aggressive activity of the infant or of the adult who has regressed to the oral stage. In like manner, soiling or feces retention express aggression in the anal stage of development.

The id, then, became the psychic representation of the sexual and aggressive drives and their many derivatives. These drives are present from birth. The id is considered as comprising the entire original psychic apparatus of the individual. The ego and superego later differentiate themselves, grow out of the id, and become separate functional entities.

Impulses of the id are not fused, organized, disciplined, or controlled. The id is subordinate only to the pleasure principle. A need is at its id source a demand for immediate gratification and operates by the primary process (see Chapter 2).

Freud thought that the superego did not begin to differentiate itself in any clear fashion until the fifth or sixth year of life. The ego, however, gradually starts to develop from about the sixth month onward. Frustration by the external environment is the factor that leads to the growth of the ego functions of the psyche. When the environment has consistently said "no" under certain circumstances to the demands of the id for immediate gratification, the infant begins to differentiate between himself and external reality and between the id impulses which external reality gratifies (pleasure) and the id impulses which external reality frustrates (pain). This "precipitate" of experience, these growing reality perceptions and the infant's adjustments to the perceptions, come to constitute the ego. The ego is the executant for the drives, the mediator between the id and the external environment. It is the "I," the self, the aspect of personality responsible for perceiving, knowing, thinking, feeling, choosing, and the kind of doing that follows perception of the outside world. The ego controls the crude impulses of the id and distributes psychic energy in what are thought by the ego's perceptions to be those ways which will insure maximal pleasure.

Like the ego, the superego is a function of personality which grows out of the id, but not until around the ages of five or six years. More specifically, the superego, according to Freud, develops as a result of the Oedipal conflict. In the pre-Oedipal period the child may be considered largely amoral. He does what he is told to do contrary to his own id impulses only because he (or, in Freudian terms, his ego) perceives the punishing effects of the environment (usually in the form of his parents) as a greater source of pain than the frustration of his id impulses. When threat of punishment from external sources is removed for the pre-Oedipal child, however, his id impulses take over, unrestrained by internal sanctions. But after about the fifth year, morality begins to become an internal matter with the child and proceeds to develop until a point of considerable stabilization is often reached at about the age of ten.

This internalization of the parental point of view by the child comes about through the process of identification with the parents in doing battle with the id impulses which emerge in the Oedipal struggle. Because the child becomes so frightened by his own impulses to kill the one parent and by the anticipated retaliation (castration) for his desire to engage in sexual activity with the other parent, he comes to see no alternative but to join forces with his parents in repressing these dangerous Oedipal urges. As he increasingly does so, the internalized "parent," the superego, comes into being.

As we parenthetically mentioned earlier, the superego corresponds roughly to what we consider "conscience." Contrary to the usual conception of "conscience," however, Freud believed the superego to be largely unconscious. As conceived by Freud, the superego becomes a kind of never-sleeping censor which critically examines the impulses of the id and the various activities of the ego, ready to pounce upon and punish what is judged to be "immoral" and to reward with self-praise and self-love all desirable or virtuous thoughts, feelings, and action.

Since the superego is based upon childish perceptions of reality and is largely the internalization of whatever the parental authority figure seemed to evaluate as "bad," the moral reactions of the individual are likely to contain many irrationalities. An important part of the analyst's role during the process when the patient is reliving his childhood experiences in the analytic setting is to help him to make a more realistic and rational evaluation of morality.

One clinically important aspect of the disapproving superego that Freud pointed out is worthy of special note. It is rather obvious to the individual who feels guilty that he has violated his conscience, his conception of morality. By no means so obvious, however, are inferiority feelings as signals of the violation of superego dictates. Freud showed how such feelings commonly arise from unconscious disapproval of the superego. The individual may consciously give himself all sorts of apparent reasons for a feeling of inadequacy, failure, low self-esteem, but the probable unconscious (and real) reason is that he has violated the instructions of his superego. According to some now unconscious memories of internalized parental dictates, the individual feels inferior as a "bad boy."

The introduction of the structural theory of the psyche led to a number of other changes in Freudian theory and in the emphasis of clinical practice. One of the important theoretical changes was in Freud's view of the nature of anxiety. Anxiety, according to Freud's original theories, resulted from the accumulation of undischarged libido which was then somehow (by a method unexplained) transformed into anxiety. In 1926, Freud abandoned this idea and suggested instead that anxiety appeared in two sets of circumstances, which he referred to as "traumatic situations" and "danger situations." He considered anxiety itself, as a basic reaction pattern, was biologically inherited, not culturally acquired. The first situational instigation of the hereditary reaction of anxiety are the traumatic situations where the psyche is overwhelmed by an influx of stimuli too great to handle. The prototype of traumatic situational anxiety is the birth experience (an idea much more extensively developed later by Otto Rank, who proposed it as the source of all neuroses—see Chapter 4). Other such traumatic instigations could also emerge in the life of the individual, but mainly such experiences are confined to childhood when the ego is relatively weak and undeveloped.

As the ego of the child develops, he learns to recognize and anticipate situations which contain potential trauma and to react to the anticipation of them with anxiety. This type of recognized or anticipated danger (as distinguished from the overwhelming, unhandled influx of stimuli in the traumatic type of anxiety), Freud called signal anxiety. The ego of the child reacts with anxiety to the anticipated danger: thus anxiety is a signal of impending danger for which the ego mobilizes its defenses. Because such anxiety is experienced as strong pain or discomfort (or "unpleasure," as it is often referred to in psychoanalytic writings), the ego is able to command much psychic energy from the id to deal with the situation.

There are a number of typical danger situations which Freud pointed out as occurring in sequence in the child's life and which elicit a great deal of signal anxiety. There are (1) loss of the loved object, (2) loss of the object's love, (3) loss of or injury to the genitals (loosely referred to as "castration anxiety"), (4) disapproval and punishment by the superego. The first danger situation is probably experienced by the child even before he can be said to feel so complex an emotion as love. It is the feeling of anxiety that arises from the possibility of permanent separation from the source of gratification (in the earliest experience of the infant this is the mother and her breast; anxiety probably first arises during frustration of the infant's desire to suckle, which, in turn, brings realization that the breast is separate from himself and his desires and, hence, subject to loss).

The second danger situation is sensed with accompanying anxiety by the child somewhere around the age of 18 months. It comes with the realization by the child that the gratification of his desires is dependent upon the love and good-will of the significant persons in his environment. The discovery of the importance of the love of the significant persons for the continuance of gratification arises, like the earlier form of signal anxiety, out of frustration. In this instance, frustration is perceived by the ego of the child (whether this is objectively true or not) as withdrawal of the significant person's (still, usually, the mother's) love.

Toward the end of the third year of life, as the child moves into the phallic stage of development, the new focus of anxiety becomes his genitals. Frustration and punishment come to center in his newly-discovered source of gratification. He now fears that the significant persons in his environment will destroy this source of pleasure.

The final typical danger situation brought out by Freud comes, of course, with the development of the superego after the age of five or six years. Here the signal of danger comes from within. The threats of punishment which formerly came from the significant persons in the external environment now come from the child's internalization of these persons in the form of his superego.

Freud held that all of these dangers persist unconsciously, at least to some degree, throughout the life of the individual. The relative importance of each danger varies from person to person. Not only is some degree of each type of anxiety found in normal adults, but a high amount of one or more of the types is observable in every emotionally disturbed individual.

With the introduction of the structural hypothesis of the psyche in the early twenties, the main focus of psychoanalysis changed from concentration on the vicissitudes of the libido to centering of attention on manifestations of anxiety. In the earlier theory, as we have brought out, Freud felt that the psychoneuroses were a result of libidinal fixations at the various pregenital stages, and, hence, the principal concern of the clinical analyst was to undo fixations and to help patients adequately to discharge libido through mature, genital channels. Such earlier concern about the activities of the libido has not been entirely displaced by explorations of anxiety, but there is considerably less emphasis on the detailed and almost exclusive tracing of infantile sexual development. Stated in another way, the almost undivided concern of Freud and his followers with unconscious instinctive development (then felt to be entirely sexual) has been broadened to include a great deal of concern with the ego and its failures, especially as manifested through anxiety. What was largely a psychology of the id has been expanded to make room also for a psychology of the ego.

Freud also came to distinguish three types of anxiety: real or objective anxiety, neurotic anxiety, and moral anxiety. In objective anxiety, the source of the danger is external to the individual. He is threatened, for example, with a loss of his job or his wife or his house or his life. In neurotic anxiety, the threat of danger resides in the id. The person is anxious about being overwhelmed by an uncontrollable urge to commit some act or think some thought which his ego defines as harmful. Moral anxiety is identified as a threat from the superego: that is, anxiety about being punished by one's conscience for doing or thinking something which is contrary to the moral standards the person holds.

The foregoing discussion of the Freudian conception of anxiety may be misleading in several ways that we must try to avoid. First, it must be realized that the individual is almost never accurately aware (other than through the help of the therapist in the treatment setting) of the real sources of his anxiety. In neurotic anxiety, for example, the individual may say that he does not care to learn to dance because he thinks dancing is sinful. But unconsciously he may be afraid that in a situation of close contact with a member of the opposite sex, his id impulses (in this case, the sexual impulse) will overwhelm him and lead him to make overt sexual advances. Or, in moral anxiety, the individual may say that he will not learn to swim because it is a futile expenditure of energy. He may unconsciously, however, feel that in such a situation his superego will seize the opportunity of punishing him for his sins by causing him to drown.

Second, such distinctions among types of anxiety (objective, neurotic, moral) were made by Freud largely for the convenience of study and discussion. He realized that in actual life situations, two or more of the types are generally blended.

Third, the emphasis on anxiety in emotional disturbance should not be taken to mean that Freud thought all anxiety was pathological. Quite to the contrary, Freud contended that only by anxiety could the individual learn to become aware of dangers from within and without and thus proceed with normal development. A person without anxiety would be unable to learn how to fend off external dangers and would be at the mercy of every instinctual impulse that arose within him.

The three chief forms taken by what Freud called neurotic anxiety are (1) free-floating, (2) phobic, and (3) panic. The free-floating type of anxiety is characteristic of the "nervous" person who is constantly apprehensive about impending disaster. The anxiety is often vague and unfixed, or, if temporarily centered on something, quite transitory. Such a person, according to Freud's theory, is actually afraid of his own id. He is constantly apprehensive of the possibility that aggressive and/or sexual impulses will overwhelm his ego controls. He is not conscious, however, of this source of his anxiety.

The phobic type of anxiety derives from the same unconscious source (fear of instinctual forces) as free-floating anxiety, but is characterized by specific, intense, irrational fear. The outstanding attribute of the phobia is that the person's anxiety is out of all proportion to the actual danger in the object or situation to which the apprehension is attached. The person may have a phobia about closed places like small rooms, trains, elevators (claustrophobia); open spaces like fields, large dance-halls or auditoriums (agrophobia); high places like tall buildings, cliffs, airplanes (acrophobia); or mice, birds, snakes, water, bugs, and practically every other thing imaginable.

In each instance, the person can give a more or less plausible reason for his phobic reaction to the particular object or situation ("mice bite"; "bugs carry germs"; "elevators break down"; etc.), but the objective danger is either imaginary or very slight in relation to the degree of fear manifested. Freud found in analytical treatment of patients that the particular objects to which phobias are attached represent some temptation to or association with instinctual gratification. An obvious example would be the association of snakes with the phallic symbol: hence, fear of snakes would be associated unconsciously with fear of being overwhelmed by the sexual impulse. Moral anxiety, Freud pointed out, is often an additional complication of the neurotic anxiety of the phobia, for the feared id impulse would be, if expressed, contrary to the moral standards of the individual.

Panic anxiety apparently arises when the individual senses that his id impulses are about to break through the controls he has assembled. The person feels panic when this is about to happen. He may fully act out the sexual or aggressive impulses (for example, commit rape, "shoot up the town," jump in front of a passing automobile), or he may discharge the id impulse in some less extreme way (steal from the corner grocery, "tell off" the boss, get drunk, or use aggressive or sexual language). The person temporarily rids himself of excessive and unendurably painful anxiety by doing (more or less) what the id demands. Such panic reactions (unless the form of acting out is very mild) usually evoke punishment from the environment, but such punishment is often welcomed by the individual who has panicked. The id impulses he was unable to control will now be controlled, he feels with relief, by external forces; and the guilt feelings which arise from his superego regarding his "bad" actions are mollified by punishment. Hence, both neurotic and moral anxiety feelings are thus relieved by the administering of external punishment. The simplest illustration of this is the child who acts out "being bad" until he is punished and then proceeds contentedly with his play after punishment has been administered.

The centering of attention on anxiety and the ego's role in handling anxiety led to a closer examination of the defenses the ego normally and abnormally develops against the id impulses. Freud noted that there were the general defenses, such as a change in focus of attention, the formation of a fantasy, the furtherance of a safer and better-controlled id impulse in place of the feared one, and the neutralization of the energy of the dangerous drive. There are other more specific defense mechanisms used by the ego against the impulses of the id. While lists of these mechanisms vary among

Freudians, some of the most common are repression, rationalization, projection, introjection, regression, turning against the self, isolation, thought dissociation, reaction formation, and denial of reality. All of these defense mechanisms operate to some degree in normal behavioral development and functioning as well as in pathological conditions. Although we shall briefly discuss each mechanism singly, they often function in plurality.

The defense mechanism first recognized by Freud, and still considered the most basic, is repression. Repression is the activity of the ego which keeps the undesirable id impulse (or any feeling, wish, memory, or fantasy associated with it) from entering consciousness. Freud believed that the repressed material continues to be charged with a cathexis of psychic energy which constantly presses toward fulfillment. The ego, on the other side, maintains the repression by a counter-cathexis, an expenditure of energy opposed to the id impulse. If the cathexis increases in strength or the counter-cathexis weakens, the repressed material will emerge into consciousness. This may happen in several ways, one of which we just discussed as panic anxiety. In sleep (in the form of dreams) and in such toxic states as acute alcoholism, there is also a temporary reduction of the ego's counter-cathexis and, hence, the partial emergence of repressed id impulses. Severe frustration can also bring an increase in id cathexis and a decrease in ego counter-cathexis. Puberty is also notable for bringing an increase in the intensity of the sexual drive (and possibly also the aggressive drive) with resulting break-through of id material that had been successfully repressed in childhood.

Another common defense mechanism is rationalization. When an undesirable id impulse moves into consciousness, the ego quickly changes the nature of the thought or feeling in order to make it more acceptable. If, as a result of an aggressive impulse of destruction for a hated business associate, an individual breaks a confidence the associate made to him and gets the associate fired for some misdemeanor, his ego cannot bear to face the real motivation for his action. He rationalizes. That is, he finds ego-comforting things to say to himself (and perhaps others) about his behavior; he finds "good" reasons to substitute for the real reasons: morality comes before friendship; confidentiality should not stand in the way of justice; "it hurt me more than it did him"; loyalty to the company comes ahead of loyalty to a friend; "I did it for his own good, because remaining unpunished would have led him to worse actions in the future"; "he is more fortunate than the rest of us, for we are still stuck in this horrible place"; etc. A rationalization is likely to contain some truth in general and possibly even in the particular situation (otherwise the ego couldn't be convinced of the "truth" of a rationalization). It is, however, not relevant to the person's actual motive for doing something. The ego is thus protected from coming "face to face" with the real motive.

A third type of defense mechanism is projection. Here the individual protects his ego from recognition of an undesirable id impulse by relocating the impulse in another person. *A* is projecting when he imputes to *B* the particular impulse which he, *A*, unconsciously feels. The woman, for example, who is fighting to keep repressed a strong desire to engage in illicit sexual relations may protect her ego from being overwhelmed by such an id impulse by projecting the impulse to men as a group. Every male then becomes for this woman a potential rapist and, hence, to be avoided in all but the most public and protected situations.

Introjection is the reverse of projection. Here the ego defends itself against the unconscious pressures of the id by identifying itself with another person. If our woman of the preceding paragraph identifies herself with a seductive movie actress, for example, she can partially achieve wish fulfillment by this route and thus temporarily reduce her libidinal cathexis. By taking in (introjecting) the sexy actress, she partially fulfills her sex wish by "being" the actress in the embrace of the hero. She still, however, successfully keeps out of consciousness the fact that she even has such a sexual desire.

A fifth mechanism of defense is regression. We have already discussed this process in Chapter 2 in connection with the early Freudian theory of infantile sexuality and accompanying pathological developments. It is, in addition, often employed as a means of protecting the ego from being overwhelmed by id impulses. If the ego is unable because of severe anxiety to handle adjustment problems at the genital level, for example, there may be a reverting of a great deal of libinal energy to, say, the anal stage. Such a person might be one who has repressed all sexual feeling in a genital sense (becoming frigid or impotent), has largely isolated himself from his fellow human beings (especially of the opposite sex), and has devoted himself exclusively to the life of a sculptor. An example of a less extreme and more transitory regression to an oral point of libidinal fixation would be the angry person who "cools off" by smoking a cigarette (thus checking the aggressive id impulse).

A defense mechanism which is generally seen only in children and the emotionally disturbed is called turning against the self. If the child feels an aggressive impulse toward some respected (and feared) person like a teacher or a parent and dares not express (or even consciously admit) such an impulse, he may strike or berate himself. Often introjection accompanies turning against the self. The child is, in effect, temporarily being the hated parent and thus striking the parent as he strikes himself. But the ego is spared, and the aggressive impulse is reduced without being openly directed toward the parent.

Seventh in our list of ego defenses is what Freud called isolation of affect. It may be considered a particular type of repression, where memory or fantasy of some painful past experience is readily accessible to the consciousness, but the feeling (generally pain) has been dissociated. That is, instead of a complete repression of some past event, only the emotion connected with the event is kept out of consciousness. Thus, the ego is protected from the id impulse by having the emotional power of the impulse repressed. By analogy, the usual form of complete repression is to remove from consciousness the whole memory of some "horrible monster" in the id. By the mechanism of isolation, the monster appears in consciousness, but all his horror has been removed.

A somewhat related form of ego defense (which Freud also referred to as "isolation," but for which, to avoid confusion, we use another term) is thought dissociation. It is marked by momentary "mental blankness." When the ego wishes to protect itself from a thought that carries with it dangerous id impulses, it dissociates this thought from thoughts that preceded it and thoughts which follow it. Thus deprived of associations, the dreaded thought will have difficulty re-entering consciousness.

Reaction formation is a ninth and allegedly much more common defense mechanism. As brought out in Chapter 2, ambivalence often exists regarding persons with whom the individual interacts. One of the ambivalent feelings (the feared one) is rendered unconscious and kept that way by an overemphasis on the other. This is reaction formation. The ego is protected from the threatened aggressive impulses of the id toward the child, the parent, the mate, and other significant persons by *conscious* feelings of love, protection, tenderness, gentleness, and so on.

The tenth and final defense mechanism which we shall discuss is denial of reality. Such denial is most readily observable in severe pathological conditions. For example, it is common for persons who have suffered paralysis as a result of a brain injury to deny the reality of their paralysis. Even if the paralyzed limb is brought into their area of vision, they "don't see" the limb at all, or fail to recognize its paralyzed state, or even claim that it is the limb of some person other than the patient. The ego is thus being protected from facing the disagreeable state of reality: namely, the paralysis. Less obviously than in this example of objectively recognizable paralysis, the ego uses the denial mechanism to protect itself from external stimuli that are associated with dangerous id impulses. Denial of reality may be considered a special form of repression that prevents admission to consciousness of external stimuli that point to the existence of dread id impulses.

It is not possible for us to proceed in even summary fashion with the application of the later Freudian theories to the specific pathological conditions met with in the clinic. We must confine ourselves to an indication of the broad outline of change in emphasis that the new theories made in Freudian treatment of emotional disturbances. In general, either excessive frustration or over-indulgence in the early years of life lead to the development of a weak ego, and a weak ego makes for serious pathological difficulties. A strongly frustrated or overindulged ego does not learn its main task of mediating between the id and external reality. In severe and constant frustration, the id impulses are given little opportunity for even indirect satisfaction, and, hence, the full psychic energy available to the ego is utilized in the task of repression. This leaves the ego ineffectual for dealing with external reality. In over-indulgence, the id impulses are easily gratified, and the ego never sufficiently develops. This is true because it is only out of meeting frustration (in moderate amounts) and learning how to handle it that the ego develops its strengths and skills in relation to external reality. The overindulged, like the overly frustrated, id produces a sick, weak ego.

Just as the ego can become seriously incapacitated, problems can develop in the individual's superego. The whole Oedipal struggle may not be successfully resolved. The superego, aware of strong unresolved lust for one parent and destructive tendencies toward the other, may be exceedingly harsh in its judgment of every act of the individual. Such a person is constantly ridden with guilt and inferiority feelings. He tends to be a neurotic perfectionist with a self-evaluation of being a miserable failure (whatever may be his external successes). Or the Oedipal struggle may misfire in the other direction: an unduly lenient superego may develop. This type of individual will develop pathological patterns as a result of insufficient moral standards. The extreme form of this latter malady would be the so-called sociopathic or psychopathic personality.

When a relatively stable balance among the ego, id, and superego is achieved, the existing state, in Freudian terms, constitutes the person's character structure. If the person seems relatively happy and well-adapted to his environment, his character structure may be considered healthy or normal. If his capacity for pleasure is relatively restricted and his adaptation to his environment is relatively impaired, he is said to have a pathological character structure (or a character disorder or a character neurosis).

A psychoneurosis, as distinguished from a character neurosis, may be understood in terms of the later Freudian theories as the ego's failure to control the id impulses. None of the ego's ordinary defenses are sufficiently strong to prevent a break-through of undesirable id impulses. The ego, in the course of an acute and desperate conflict with the id, works out what Freud referred to as a "compromise formation." The compromise formation unconsciously expresses both the id impulse and the ego reaction and constitutes what, in contemporary parlance, is called a psychosomatic symptom. Vomiting, for example, may represent a pregnant mother's unacceptable id impulse to destroy an unwanted child and the ego's partial success in preventing the expression of this impulse. That is, the compromise formation of vomiting gives partial vent to the id's desire to get rid of this child, but also represents the ego's success in curbing full expression of (and even consciousness of) the destructive impulse. (It is not here suggested that there may not be physiological reasons of an entirely different sort for vomiting in some instances of its occurrence in pregnancy.) In addition to such psychosomatic expressions of compromise formations between id and ego in psychoneurosis, there is the intensive and habitual employment of one or more of the special defense mechanisms we have discussed (such as regression, projection, denial of reality, introjection, etc.).

The success of psychoanalysis in the treatment of the psychoneuroses and the character neuroses varies with many factors according to Freud and his followers. In general, the greatest success seems to be obtained with young adults and with persons who feel the greatest dissatisfaction with or discomfort in the neurotic states. Failure is by no means rare even in these groups.

Although Freud's theories grew chiefly out of his observations in the course of an active clinical practice, psychoanalytic therapy also followed the pattern of theoretical development. When Freud first discovered the influence of the unconscious on the behavior of the individual, therapy consisted primarily in bringing repressed material into consciousness. Many psychoanalysts today remain strongly under the influence of the early theory and still insist that the main job of an analysis is that of rendering unconscious content and process conscious. As Freud himself (considerably greater in flexibility than some of his followers) developed the structural theory of the psyche, however, he increasingly realized that the ego must undergo changes in order to become capable of handling the repressed material brought up in the free associations. The emphasis in therapy, therefore, came to be placed more and more on resistance (the ego defenses as they related to the individual's inability to face and handle unconscious wishes which appeared in the course of the analysis) and transference as the means of overcoming such resistance and helping the ego to utilize psychic energy which had been going into the major ego defenses (especially repression). The relationship of the analyst to the patient was increasingly recognized as essential as the effect of the newer Freudian theories came to be felt in psychoanalytic practice. Much of the recent psychoanalytic work has dealt not only with transference (that is, the displacements of feelings from significant persons in the patient's past to the therapist), but counter-transference (that is, the displacements of past feelings of the therapist's relationships with others to the present patient).

Freud in his later work emphasized the corrective influence of the objective, non-evaluative attitude of the analyst. As the patient relives his childhood experiences in the therapeutic situation, change in his attitudes is effected because he has never before experienced objective reactions to his behavior. The patient will be able to face what he formerly repressed because of the censure of significant persons in his past. While insight is still considered important, the corrective emotional experience of the therapy itself has been increasingly stressed as the means whereby the individual's ego can have the strength to handle the formerly repressed material in an integrative fashion.

It should be realized that we have tried to confine our discussion of Freudian psychoanalysis largely to the theories of normal and pathological behavior and to the clinical procedures related to these theories. There are many other theories and applications of psychoanalysis made by Freud and his followers. Freud turned his attention to numerous aspects of society and activities of various groups within society. He and others of his persuasion have made provocative studies of art, science, literature, religion, war, and many other social phenomena. Such matters as these, however, are out of the range of our consideration.

Summary

From 1900 to 1923, Freud developed three somewhat separate theories of the general nature of the psyche. The last of these, called the structural hypothesis, brought about many important changes in psychoanalytic theory and practice. Freud expanded his conception of the basic instincts to include an aggressive drive (death instinct) as well as the sexual drive. The id, according to the structural hypothesis, became the psychic representation of these basic drives or instincts and their derivatives. The ego is the mediator between the id and external reality, and the superego comprises the individual's moral precepts and ideal aspirations. The ego begins to form about the sixth month of life, but the superego does not develop until the fifth or sixth year, as a result of the Oedipal struggle.

Later Freudian theory and practice concentrated much attention on the role of anxiety. Freud proposed that anxiety appeared in two sets of circumstances, "traumatic situations" and "danger situations." The birth trauma stands as a prototype of the former. Typical danger situations which evoke signal anxiety are loss of the loved object, loss of the object's love, loss of or injury to the genitals, and disapproval and punishment by the superego. Freud held that these typical dangers and their accompanying anxiety persist unconsciously throughout the life of the individual. He also distinguished objective or reality anxiety, neurotic anxiety, and moral anxiety. Neurotic anxiety was further subdivided into free-floating, phobic, and panic.

The centering of attention on anxiety and the ego's role in handling anxiety led to a closer examination of the defenses the ego develops against id impulses. Ten special defense mechanisms are considered: repression, rationalization, projection, introjection, regression, turning against the self, isolation, thought dissociation, reaction formation, and denial of reality. All of these defense mechanisms operate in both normal and abnormal behavioral development and functioning.

One of the results of the new Freudian theories was that in practice psychoanalysis became less exclusively a study of unconscious processes and developed increasing interest in the activities of the ego and superego. Many pathologies could now be understood in terms of the malfunctioning of these latter two aspects of personality. In general, distinction was now made in Freudian terms between a character neurosis (where the balance among the ego, id, and superego is such that the person's capacity for pleasure is relatively restricted and his adaptation to his environment is relatively impaired) and a psychoneurosis (partial failure of the ego to control the id impulses). As psychoanalytic clinical practice has proceeded increasingly with applications of ego psychology, more and more emphasis has been placed on the importance of the relationship between the analyst and the patient and on the corrective influence of the relatively objective therapeutic situation itself.

Selected Readings

Fenichel, Otto, *The Psychoanalytic Theory of the Neuroses.* New York: Norton, 1945.

Freud, Anna, *The Ego and the Mechanisms of Defense* (translated by C. M. Baines). New York: Int. Univs., 1946.

Freud, Sigmund, *A General Introduction to Psychoanalysis* (translated by Joan Riviere). New York: Garden City, 1943.

———, *Beyond the Pleasure Principle* (translated by James Strachey). New York: Liveright, 1950.

———, *New Introductory Lectures on Psychoanalysis* (translated by J. H. Sprott). New York: Norton, 1933.

———, *The Ego and the Id* (translated by Joan Riviere). London: Hogarth Press, 1935.

———, *The Problem of Anxiety* (translated by H. A. Bunker). New York: Norton, 1936.

Jones, Ernest, *The Life and Work of Sigmund Freud,* Vols. II and III. New York: Basic Books, 1955 and 1957.

CHAPTER 4

Deviations in Psychoanalysis: I

As we noted in Chapter 3, Freud showed considerable flexibility in his own thinking and was never hesitant to change his theories in the light of newly-discovered facts. But he was often less than generous in the consideration he gave to new and independent hypotheses developed by some of his followers. Some of the men Freud attracted, however, were ill-suited for the role of compliant pupil. The result was a succession of schisms in the psychoanalytic movement. In this chapter, we'll consider six foremost pupils of Freud who departed from his teachings and, in varying degrees, set up systems of their own.

A. ADLER

Alfred Adler was the first of Freud's pupils to break with the master (in 1911). Adler rejected the sexual etiology of neurosis and contended that feelings of inferiority were the true cause. Adler stated that Freud and his followers were misled by the "jargon" of neurotic patients into believing that sex lay at the root of their difficulties. Patients, Adler held, were really expressing a compulsion in the direction of the "masculine goal" by their sexual fantasies and sexual feelings. Masculinity represents strength and power in Adler's system, and femininity symbolizes weakness and inferiority. "Masculine protest" is common in both men and women (but especially the latter) and is a striving for power. Instead of sex, according to Adler, the search for power determines human actions and development.

Everyone develops some sense of inferiority, Adler pointed out, because he is born completely helpless and remains relatively weak and dependent during a long childhood. Such basic inferiority can be exaggerated by body or organ defects (whether real or imaginary), by having older and more powerful siblings, parental rejection or neglect, and by many other factors. One way to cope with feelings of inferiority is by compensatory action: gaining power to overcome the sense of weakness. This aggressive or masculine reaction often leads to considerable success in terms of recognized achievement in some area of life, some accomplishment of power over one's fellows. The second way of coping with feelings of inferiority is more easily recognizable as neurotic: the submissive or feminine patterns of denial or retreat. Such retreat or denial may take the form of fantasies, psychosomatic illnesses, projections, rationalizations, denials of reality, and other defense mechanisms which we considered within the Freudian frame of reference in Chapter 3.

Adler felt that a person's development was conditioned by his social environment rather than by biological forces and insisted that an individual could be analyzed and understood in terms of his present purposes or life goals rather than in terms of his infantile past. Adlerian analysis is undertaken in terms of each individual's "life plan" or "life style." Since everyone's life style is in some ways unique, Adler came to refer to his system as "individual psychology." Once the particular life style of the individual is fully understood, the job of the therapist is to re-educate the patient to what are believed to be healthier patterns and goals. Adler emphasized social feelings and community interests and service as goals that therapy could put in the place of less desirable strivings for power.

Sex to Adler was simply a handy weapon available to the individual in his struggle to gain power over others. He saw the Oedipus complex as being of secondary importance and symptomatic of the struggle of the child (in actuality or in fantasy) to gain power over the parent. Only the pampered child, according to Adler, fails to resolve his Oedipal conflict as a result of his timidity about extending his sexual power to someone other than the over-indulging parent.

Adlerian therapists (of whom a fair number exists in New York, Chicago, Los Angeles, and principal European cities) follow Adler's example in minimizing unconscious forces and in exploring past events only insofar as they cast initial insight on the patient's life style. Just as the unconscious and its sexual manifestations are not stressed, correspondingly less emphasis (than that of the Freudians) is placed on the importance of transference. It is only when strong feelings are displaced from significant persons in the patient's life onto the therapist in a way that blocks therapeutic progress that the individual psychologist gives any attention to transference phenomena.

Adler was the first psychotherapist to place high value on the social relationship between the therapist and the patient. He believed that this relationship could serve as a re-educative bridge to other relationships. He held that all individuals who fail are deficient in concern and love for their fellow human beings, and he devoted most of his energy in therapy to the attempt at increasing the social interest of the patient. The disturbed person, Adler thought, had a private and irrational meaning for life that stops short of deep and positive feeling for others. The therapist's job, then, as Adler saw it, was to help the individual to substitute realistic for unrealistic life goals and to instill social interest and feeling.

As already implied, Adler's treatment procedures were greatly different from those he had learned from Freud. He dispensed with the couch and substituted face to face sitting positions. He assumed an active, teaching role as therapist. He used dream interpretation largely to cast further light on present life style and future life goals. Interruptions of the patient were frequent, for Adler conceived the therapist's responsibility that of pointing out self-deceptive tendencies to the patient. Hence, free association gave way to a therapist-directed interview. Patients were usually seen three or four times a week (compared with the Freudian five or six), and a much shorter total term of treatment (than the Freudian) was the general rule.

B. STEKEL

Wilhelm Stekel broke with Freud after Adler and shortly before Jung. He lacked both the systematic organization in his writings and the temperament in his interpersonal relations to develop a well-knit school of followers. He has, however, had some influence (sometimes uncredited) on the development of psychotherapy in the

United States. Stekel's contributions were primarily in technique, rather than theory, but he made several original theoretical changes in psychoanalysis. Stekel's intuitive skills in dream interpretation influenced Freud in his adoption of various symbols. Stekel was also a pioneer observer and writer on the subject of sex, normal and pathological, and many of his views hold up well in the light of modern sex research.

The patient's current conflicts were as important as past conflicts in the Stekelian approach. Like Adler, Stekel felt that the Freudians were too preoccupied with the patient's past to give proper attention to the present. In some cases, Stekel contended, the patient could be helped without any recourse to the distant past. Even in those instances where past conflicts were important, current conflicts, he felt, also needed a great deal of the analyst's attention.

Stekel anticipated some of the recent Freudian emphasis on character analysis and counter-transference (see Chapter 3). He asserted that the future of psychoanalysis rested in the development of a growing understanding of the character structure of the patient and emphasized a close relationship between the specific personality characteristics of the patient and the main trends and tendencies of his psychoneurotic condition. Although he did not discuss counter-transference as such, Stekel frequently stressed that the personality of the analyst is the decisive factor in the progress of the therapy. He maintained that the personality of the therapist, rather than his particular method, is of greatest curative significance.

Stekel stated that his emphasis on his role as a therapist and his responsibility to try to cure the patients who came to him was the factor that sharply distinguished his procedures from those of Freud. The latter, Stekel said, seemed to be more interested in advancing his theories and techniques than in helping a particular patient. Stekel held that Freud considered himself first a scientist and secondly a therapist and that he, Stekel, had a reversed priority. Freud's guide was mainly: "What can I learn from this patient about the psychological nature of human beings?" Stekel's standard was: "How can I cure this patient?"

However much truth one wishes to place in Stekel's evaluation of Freud, he seemed to have a correct perspective of his own chief focus of interest. His concentration on the curative process as such seems to account for most of his innovations in technique. He came to take a more and more active role in the therapeutic process in an effort to achieve a cure more speedily and effectively. Appropriately enough, Stekel referred to his procedures as "active analytic psychotherapy."

The analyst, as Stekel conceived him, is an active partner throughout therapy. He collaborates from the outset with the patient in the interpretation of his free associations and dreams. He may intervene in the course of the patient's association to suggest more detailed discussion of what the therapist considers a significant point. Or he may recommend the dropping of a certain line of association as nonfruitful or indicative of resistance. Stekel emphasized the importance of intuitive listening in the therapist. He believed that intuition was a combination of sympathy and imaginative insight and could be acquired by special effort and training. By the use of intuition, Stekel maintained, the therapist could be aware of the appropriate timing of interventions to break down the patient's resistances to insight.

Stekel did not even avoid occasional exhortation and direct advice, but he stressed the patient's own responsibility in all decision making. Although Stekel himself was apparently quite authoritarian in his attack on patients' resistances, his followers (of whom Emil A. Gutheil is the best known in the United States) tend to be more permissive and objective in their approach to active analysis.

Much of Stekel's intuitive analysis was focused on the dreams brought in by his patients. He felt that his own demonstrable skill in dream interpretation was no particular gift, but, like other aspects of intuition, something that could be developed by an analyst who devoted himself to the task. Stekel was primarily interested in current attitudes and responses of the patient as revealed in dreams and was concerned with past dream events only in the sense of throwing light on the patient's basic characterological difficulties. His basic agreement with Adler is here apparent.

Although Stekel recognized transference as a part of every analysis, he felt it seldom became a major problem in active analytic psychotherapy because the therapist is constantly demolishing patients' illusions and their childish displacements of emotion. He felt that enough positive transference would automatically develop toward a successful active therapist (simply out of gratitude of the patient for improvements felt by him) to help the patient to face some of the difficult tasks of the analysis. But, since the active analyst foresees a limited relationship (rarely more than six months was required by Stekel's methods), he does not encourage the patient to develop the fantasy of a permanent romantic relationship (which, Stekel held, is often the case in classical psychoanalysis).

As already indicated, present-day followers of Stekel have not held rigidly to his teachings. They have, in fact, contended that the essence of the Stekelian approach is activity and flexibility, that many of Stekel's ideas have been adopted freely into current psychoanalysis of other "schools," and that they themselves feel free to adopt ideas from various non-Stekelian sources. Most contemporary active psychoanalytic therapists do not hold rigidly to the six-month limitation on the length of therapy, are less authoritarian than Stekel in their approach to patients, and place less emphasis on the strictly intuitive aspects of analytic interpretation.

C. JUNG

The deviations of Adler and Stekel were, as we have seen, in the general direction of greater directness and simplicity in theories and techniques than those expounded by Freud. The departure of Carl Jung led to the development of a system more esoteric and complicated than that of Freud.

Jung's complete break with Freud came in 1912, but he had not been as wholehearted in his acceptance of the Freudian views from the very beginning as had some of Freud's followers. Jung's increasingly independent ideas reached a point of irreparable rupture with his publication, in 1912, of a new interpretation of the nature of the libido (*The Psychology of the Unconscious*).

It is interesting to observe that in terms of our own historical perspective a substantial portion of the difference in the Freudian and Jungian conceptions of libido seems to be a matter of words and not basic concepts. The "primal" libido, according to Jung, is undifferentiated energy, a universal "life urge." Early in the history of the human race, however, Jung said, the libido was primarily sexual in nature, but became desexualized in the course of human evolution and could no longer be reconverted into sexual energy. Jung particularly rejected the notion that the sucking of the infant is any way sexual in nature. But Freud had said (see Chapter 2) that there were four stages of development of libidinal fixation, characterized by certain zones in which a major portion of psychic energy (libido) focused: the oral, anal, phallic, and genital. Since, Freud said, the same psychic energy that focuses genitally in the adult is manifesting itself in the three earlier stages, it is proper and convenient to conceive of the libido as sexual from infancy onward. Jung, on the other hand, said that this energy had a neutral quality (as a result of an evolutionary desexualizing process) and took on the characteristics of the zones into which it flowed and fixated itself: hence, the libido was hunger, not sex, at the oral stage. To paraphrase, we have this situation: Freud said the libido is observable in A, B, C, and D stages; since it is the same libido that finally reaches fruition in D (genitally fixated sex), we shall call it D (sex) from the very beginning. Jung said that the libido is an X (neutral) force that flows through various stages and that it is improper to call it by the name of any particular stage. But, by and large, the two men seemed to have the same fundamental life force in mind.

So sensitive was Freud, however, to the many resistances and condemnations of the sexual aspects of his theory that he could not have been expected to accept Jung's desexualized description of the libido. Neither he nor Jung recognized that the differences between their theories were largely semantic. And it may be that Freud was right that Jung and his followers found that a desexualized libido was both personally and publicly more palatable, especially in the concentration of Jungian interest in religious and ethical phenomena.

In like manner, Jung's interpretations of the Oedipus complex and the Electra complex (a term he used to refer to the affection of the girl for her father and jealousy toward her mother) indicate a departure from Freudian thinking which is greater in words than in substance. Jung does emphasize the early hunger-satisfying (not, he contends, sexual) pleasure that the mother provides the child, but he does admit that the love of the child for the mother develops a sexual characteristic as the infant matures. The nature of the Oedipus complex thus becomes very similar in Jung's view to that of Freud's.

Although Jung substantially adopted many of Freud's concepts, his emphasis in both theory and therapy was different from Freud's. Jung was mainly interested in the purposive, goal-striving interpretations of behavior rather than the causative sources. To this extent his point of view resembled Adler. Jung considered the Oedipus complex, for example, along with the whole sexuality of the unconscious, as a symbol with a prospective, not retrospective, reference. Although the behavior of the individual, including his Oedipal strivings, arise from an earlier mode of adaptation to life, it signifies, according to Jung, a step forward on the road to various life purposes. Unlike Adler, however, who sought to understand the specific life purposes of the unique individual, Jung visualized various collective life purposes, which strike most non-Jungians as vague, non-testable, mystical.

Jung observed that the symbolic productions of disturbed persons resembled those of primitive people. From this he speculated that there must be an hereditary portion of the mind that contained the imprints of ancestral experience. He therefore hypothesized the existence of a collective unconscious. Jung thought he could see primordial images, which he called "archetypes," in associations, fantasies, drawings and dreams. The most common of these archetypes, Jung held, were the Animus, the mate ideal of the female psyche, and the Anima, the mate ideal of the male psyche. Along with the collective unconscious (and its contained archetypes), Jung further subdivided the human psyche into the persona (the superficial social mask of the individual which he presents to others in his social relationships) and the ego (a deeper part of the psyche which is reflective of personal experiences and is partly conscious and partly unconscious).

Emotional disturbance develops in an individual, according to Jung, whenever disharmony develops among the persona, the ego, and the collective unconscious and also whenever the masculine Animus gets out of balance with the feminine Anima. Whenever a person becomes too extreme in his personality sub-type of introversion (interests centered in himself) or of extroversion (interests centered in the external world), he is also likely to become emotionally disturbed.

Jung, like Adler and Stekel, used dream interpretations chiefly for an aid to understanding current difficulties and future strivings more than past unconscious sources of psychic problems. Also similarly to the two previous deviants, Jung made free association secondary to specific focusing of the interview along lines considered significant by the therapist. Jung also contended that the quantity and quality of the therapist's interpretations should vary with the personality type of the patient: introverts need extensive, detailed, and refined interpretation, and extroverts are satisfied if the prescribed behavioral change improves their adjustment and are less interested in the dynamic causations of the change.

Jung may, with Stekel, be considered a forerunner of the contemporary emphasis in psychoanalysis on counter-transference, the analyst's own problems, and the ability of the analyst to learn from the patient. He likewise anticipated Rank and some of the later deviants in stressing the positive and creative aspects of personality which can be brought out in therapy and in seeing the constructive importance of the therapist-patient interactions.

Probably more than in any other system of psychotherapy, however, it is difficult for the outsider to see how the Jungian theory sheds much light on actual human behavior or how the theory functions in the therapeutic situation. Patients are undoubtedly helped by the interest and constructive suggestions of the Jungian therapist about current life difficulties, and Jungians show for the importance and integrity of the individual patients a respect not always so evident in some other practitioners. But just how the various metaphysical and mystical interpretations of the alleged parts of the individual's psyche contribute help to the patient is not at all clear. The system has the quality of an esoteric religion, and it seems at times to take the patient away from reality and to encourage the development of a mystical fantasy life.

The Jungian analytical psychology did not develop many followers in the United States. Indirectly, however, some of Jung's ideas have become absorbed into contemporary psychotherapy. His influence on Rank, Horney, and Fromm, and their influence in turn on the American psychoanalytic movement, has been considerable.

D. RANK

Otto Rank joined Freud's inner circle of Viennese followers while still a very young student and remained for many years one of Freud's closest associates. Around 1920, however, Rank began to experiment with short-term therapy, activity versus passivity in the analytic situation, and related technical issues. Soon thereafter he began to expound theoretical changes in psychoanalysis that grew out of his clinical innovations. A break developed between Freud and Rank, and Rank moved from Vienna to Paris (and later to New York).

Rank can in some ways be considered, with Stekel, a forerunner of the present-day advocates of short-term psychoanalytic therapy. His theories have also contributed importantly to the Philadelphia or the "functional" (as distinguished from the Freudian-based "diagnostic") school in social casework and to client-centered or non-directive therapy (to be discussed in Chapter 6). Rank's orientation also tended to emphasize social relationships in the etiology of mental illness much more than did Freud's, so he may be considered a precursor of such "dynamic-culturalists" in psychoanalysis as Horney and Fromm.

Rank's most devastating attack on established psychoanalytic theory came with his publication in 1924 of his *Trauma of Birth.* Here Rank introduced a mother-centered conception of fear, anxiety, dependency, and insecurity. He contended that the birth trauma was more important then the Oedipus complex as a source of emotional disturbance. He also questioned the passive role of the analyst in therapy and argued for a more active, flexible, and creative functioning of the analyst.

Central in the Rankian theory is the conception of the will as an expression of the positive, unifying, growing, creative aspects of the individual in his movement toward independence. Blocking the positive will are the dependency strivings of the individual—the pathological tendency to "return to the womb." The Rankian analyst analyzes the birth trauma and thus helps the individual to overcome his pathological womb-returning tendencies and to release his constructive will.

Although Rank felt the analytic hour offered the patient an opportunity to live through past experiences, especially the birth trauma, his emphasis in therapy was on the present rather than the past. The patient was encouraged to assert himself in order to strengthen his own will and, through the mobilization of constructive elements in his personality, to transfer negative expression of will (which corresponds to the Freudian concept of resistance) into positive and creative will.

Like Stekel, Rank reacted strongly against the "interminable" length of classical analyses. In fact, Rank's experimentation with specific "end-setting" or "time limit" in therapy, together with the accompanying greater activity of the therapist, were the chief technical changes out of which theoretical deviations developed.

Rank emphasized the flexible, adaptible, individual, patient-centered nature of the therapeutic process. It was in this way that he anticipated the later development of client-centered therapy. Rebelling against the rigid, pre-determined notions of the content of each analysis, Rank held that every relationship between patient and therapist should be a unique and creative process and that the patient, not the therapist, needed to point the way to his particular method of achieving self-determination and self-direction.

The degree to which such therapeutic ideals of permissive self-realization are truly practical in work with highly disturbed persons has been the subject of much disputation between Rankians and other therapists. The controversy has grown in intensity and extent with the advent of non-directive or client-centered therapy (see Chapter 6), and the facts for its resolution are not currently discernible.

E. FERENCZI

Sandor Ferenczi may be considered a Freudian deviant mainly in method rather than in theory. In his earlier explorations for improved therapeutic techniques, Ferenczi was closely associated with Otto Rank. Like Rank, Ferenczi first departed from the classical analytic techniques by taking a more active role in therapy. In his efforts to break down the resistance manifested by his patients, Ferenczi extremely extended the Freudian dictum of patient privation while in analysis. Freud had recommended sexual abstinence for the patient on the basis that the libido, deprived of sexual outlet, would concentrate itself with greater force in the past emotional experiences that were being relived in the analytic situation. The genitals, Ferenczi reasoned, were only one point of focus for the libido of the neurotic. Privation of other bodily pleasures (which therefore had some libido attachment) should, Ferenczi thought, bring all the more libido into the emotional experiences related to the analysis. He tried to persuade his patients on the basis of this hypothesis to limit to the absolute minimum such activities as eating, drinking, defecation, and urination, as well as the direct sexual outlets.

This extreme application of the privation philosophy brought violent reaction in Ferenczi's patients, and for a time he thought that the resentment and aggression thus released and directed toward him as therapist had excellent therapeutic value. After a time, however, Ferenczi became disillusioned, for he found that the hostility patients expressed was not tied in with the emotional experiences of childhood, but simply direct reaction to the difficulties of life created in the current therapeutic situation. He carried the method on for a while on a voluntary basis to see if the removal of compulsory sanctions reduced hostility toward the analyst. He finally concluded that the whole procedure was a failure.

About 1927, Ferenczi swung his experiments in psychoanalytic techniques toward the opposite extreme to stern privation: namely, love and permissiveness. In this area of technical innovation, Ferenczi achieved some lasting fame, some following, and considerable disapproval from Freud and other classical analysts. Ferenczi's changed reasoning was to the effect that neurotics are people who have never been properly loved and accepted as children by their real parents. What disturbed people most need then, as he now saw it, is a therapist who, as a substitute parent, will let them relive their childhood experiences in a completely warm, loving, permissive atmosphere.

Ferenczi was like some of the deviants before him in discovering the importance of the therapeutic relationship and of the therapist's role in that relationship. While a greater conformist in theory than the four men we have previously discussed in this chapter, Ferenczi was a greater non-conformist than any of them in some of his techniques. Just as he had been an extremist in the imposition of authoritarian asceticism, he now became an extremist in the technique of love and permissiveness. Freud was right, Ferenczi held, in his basic technique of helping the patient to relive his childhood experiences, but did not sufficiently stress the difference in the therapeutic environment in which the reliving took place. The therapist, Ferenczi said, should set himself up in as sharp a contrast as possible with the "bad" parent in relation to whom the patient developed his neurosis. The therapist should be a "good" parent who accedes to as many of the patient's wishes as possible. The therapist also, by Ferenczi's example, should admit his mistakes, blind spots, and shortcomings to demonstrate to the patient that all parents are not self-righteous, intolerant, "deity-pretending," unloving figures. By his "relaxation therapy" Ferenczi felt he opened a new world of constructive interaction for the patient.

Ferenczi's technique of permissiveness led to his acceptance (and at times active encouragement) of the patient's dramatization of childhood experiences. If the patient wanted to "act out" some phase of early childhood, for example, Ferenczi would treat him as if he were a young child and permit him to play childish games or use childish speech. He was even known to take a disturbed person who was struggling with the dramatization of some childhood conflict into his arms or lap.

As would be expected, such activities drew fire from the classical analysts, who were noted for their formality and detachment in the therapeutic situation. Freud himself was critical of Ferenczi's ideas of encouraging acting out, of giving "love," and of admitting mistakes to patients.

For an observer of today who is relatively removed from wholehearted commitment to any particular set of techniques, there seems to be both positive and negative values in Ferenczi's innovations. As Moreno has independently demonstrated (see Chapter 9), dramatization of emotional disturbances seems at times to be an effective therapeutic technique (especially in group situations). It seems doubtful, however, that its greatest value comes in individual therapeutic situations where the therapist permits himself to get emotionally involved (as Ferenczi apparently often did). The matter of "love" of the patient, too, when carried to a Ferenczi-like extreme, can evidently be a block to understanding as readily as aloofness and frigidity can. Ferenczi apparently did not understand (as Horney was later explicit in demonstrating—see Chapter 5), that love can be neurotically as well as healthily employed by the patient and the therapist. Hence, therapeutically offered "love" will not necessarily heal the patient any more than the hostility engendered by Ferenczi in his earlier methodological experiments.

Ferenczi's extreme emphasis on love, warmth, and permissiveness, did, however, gradually bring a corrective influence in many psychoanalytic circles for the opposite classical extreme of the socially distant, anonymous, coldly mysterious analyst. In like manner, Freud and some of his followers were probably too sensitive about criticism from patients and too quick to assume that any fault of an analyst pointed out by the patient was inevitably resistance and negative transference. Ferenczi did much to bring to the attention of at least some analysts that they are imperfect human beings and that it is possible that the criticism of a patient is reality-oriented. Many contemporary analysts would hold to the view that their admission of mistakes can assist, not necessarily disrupt, an analysis, but that such admission must be done judiciously and in great moderation so that the patient will not be encouraged to make hostile and defensive diversion of the analysis to the therapist's, rather than his own, problems.

Although Ferenczi himself was careful not to develop a separate theory of psychoanalysis and to precipitate an outright break with Freud, a few followers have carried on his techniques and developed some supporting theories. These theories stress the fundamental and over-riding importance of the curative effect of love and of the need of the therapist to provide love and acceptance in the therapeutic setting regardless of the hostile provocations of the patient.

F. REICH

Wilhelm Reich first broke with Freud in 1932 in a controversy over the existence of the death instinct in general and the function of such an instinct in the causation of masochism in particular. In more recent years, Reich proceeded to develop what was variously called *orgone* therapy and *vegetotherapy,* which was not only a radical departure from Freudian psychoanalysis, but from what we in this book consider psychotherapy. We shall, therefore, make no attempt to understand these later theories of Reich and shall confine ourselves to a consideration of his contributions to psychoanalysis in the special area of character analysis.

Under contemporary psychoanalytic circumstances, especially as a result of the influence of such "dynamic culturalists" as Horney, Sullivan, and Fromm, the analysis of the character structure of the patient has become fairly routine procedure. Reich, however, was the first analyst to make character a major focus of his study. Unlike the dynamic culturalists, however, who view character analysis as the main objective of therapy (because malformations of character are believed to be the heart of the neurosis), Reich viewed character analysis as a necessary obstacle-overcoming process prior to the main task of analysis. He felt the "character armor" was the major resistance put up by many patients to the analysis of their unconscious processes. Reich considered the removal of such resistance merely essential preparation for the main analysis, that is, the retracing of the vicissitudes of the libido by the process of free association. Reich, in fact, referred to the analyzing of character resistances as "education for analysis." He felt that penetration of these resistances by repeatedly calling the patient's attention to them and analyzing the sources of such negative and resistant behavior patterns as passivity, ingratiations, and over-aggressiveness, cleared the way for the release of unconscious material.

Reich was the first analyst to make considerable observation of typical postural and other physiological reaction patterns. He also pointed out how characteristic modes of response on the part of the patient (such as cynical withdrawal or acting out tendencies) can prevent effective probing of unconscious data. He showed how the ego could play one id impulse against another, so that the defensive armor could become as instinctually resistant to change and as irrational as a repressed impulse. Far from directly reflecting the libidinal structure of the patient, character by the Reichian view typically represents a reaction against powerful libidinal tendencies and, hence, is a serious block to remove from the path of the analysis.

When Reich felt that the character armor had been broken through, he would return to the more passive role of the classical analyst. In harmony with Freud's earliest formulation of the libido theory, Reich felt that the patient, no longer fettered by his character resistances, could work through the repressed infantile sexual material and thus enable the libido to make a mature (that is, genital) fixation. Reich contended that the real test of the cure of the patient was his achievement of full orgastic potency. This view can scarcely be held today with any scientific validity, for studies of schizophrenics and other highly disturbed patients indicate that some of them have full orgastic potency.

Summary

Six major deviants among the pupils of Freud were Adler, Stekel, Jung, Rank, Ferenczi, and Reich. Adler, the first to break with Freud (1911), developed what he came to call a system of individual psychology, which was based primarily on the contention that emotional disturbance arose from feelings of inferiority and represented an individual's striving for power. Adler de-emphasized sex as a factor in mental illness and stressed present life style and future life goals instead of unconscious past events. Adler also substituted a didactic, therapist-directed interview for Freudian free association with a relatively passive therapist.

Stekel is probably the least celebrated of the deviants, for he never developed a real "school" of followers. His contributions were more in technique than in theory, but he made a few contributions in the latter. From a technical standpoint, he developed what he called an "active analytic psychotherapy" in which he emphasized current as well as past conflicts, the importance of the therapist's personality and factors of counter-transference, the active intervention of the therapist, and a further development of the analytic tool of dream interpretation.

Contrasted with the more direct, simple, didactic types of deviation of Adler and Stekel, Jung's rebellion from Freudian theory and practice went in the direction of greater complications to the point of mysticism. Although bitter denunciation and counter-denunciation broke out between Jung and Freud regarding the former's desexualizing of such important Freudian concepts as the libido and the Oedipus conflict, much of the difference in these areas seems a matter of semantics rather than of substance. Jung's emphasis in both theory and therapy was different from Freud's in seeking the purposive, goal-striving interpretations of behavior rather than the causative sources. In the course of his elaborations of what he called analytical psychology, Jung developed concepts of the collective unconscious, persona, ego, animus, anima, archetypes, introverts, extroverts, etc. A few of

Jung's concepts (notably introversion and extroversion) have been adopted into the general psychological literature, but his chief lasting contribution would appear to be his focus on some of the positive and creative aspects of personality and in his influence on later deviants such as Horney and Fromm.

Rank at first experimented only with technical changes in classical analysis (including short-term therapy), but later broke with Freud and developed a new theoretical system. He made the birth trauma more significant than the Oedipus complex and, hence, centered attention on the mother, rather than the father, as most influential in the development of the individual. Rank also had a social, rather than a biological, emphasis in the theories he held about causation of both pathological and normal aspects of personality. He, like Jung, brought out the positive and creative potentialities of the individual and thought of therapy as offering the opportunity for the patient to release these potentialities (for which he used the term "will"). Rank has had a considerable influence in one framework of social casework (the "functional" school), in client-centered therapy, and, less directly, the dynamic-cultural forces in psychoanalysis.

Ferenczi, unlike the other five men discussed in this chapter, never completely broke with Freud (although Freud publicly and privately rebuked him for his deviations). He experimented at first with a more active form of authoritarianism in therapy, and then he turned to the opposite extreme of love and permissiveness. In this latter procedure, the therapist creates an environment of warmth and acceptance for the patient. This environment, because of its contrast with the neurosis-producing atmosphere of the patient's early parental home, gives him an opportunity to work through his unresolved conflicts to a mature and normal termination. In the course of such permissiveness, Ferenczi encouraged criticism of the therapist by the patient, bilateral expression of "love," and a dramatization ("acting out") of childhood difficulties. His influence has been valuable in "humanizing" the psychoanalytic process, but it is generally thought that he was impractical in his utilization of the techniques to which we have referred.

Reich, the last of the six deviants considered in this chapter, broke with Freud over the death instinct and masochism. He proceeded in later years to develop orgone therapy (vegetotherapy), which departs so radically from not only psychoanalysis, but our conception of psychotherapy, that it is not herein considered. Reich was so well known, however, for his brilliant and original analyses of character structure (done, for the most part, prior to his break with Freud) that his name is worthy of inclusion in our consideration of the non-Freudian developments of psychoanalysis.

Selected Readings

Adler, Alfred, *The Practice and Theory of Individual Psychology*. New York: Harcourt, 1924.

Ansbacher, H. L., and Rowena R. (Eds), *The Individual-Psychology of Alfred Adler*. New York: Basic Books, 1956.

Ferenczi, Sandor, *Sex in Psychoanalysis*. New York: Basic Books, 1950.

———, *Further Contributions to the Theory and Technique of Psychoanalysis*. New York: Basic Books, 1952.

Jung, Carl G., *Modern Man in Search of a Soul*. New York: Harcourt, 1933.

———, *The Practice of Psychotherapy*. New York: Pantheon, 1954.

Karpf, Fay B., *The Psychology and Psychotherapy of Otto Rank*. New York: Philosophical Lib., 1953.

Rank, Otto, *Will Therapy and Truth and Reality*. New York: Knopf, 1947.

Reich, Wilhelm, *Character Analysis*. New York: Orgone Institute, 1945.

Stekel, Wilhelm, *Compulsion and Doubt*. New York: Liveright, 1949.

———, *Technique of Analytical Psychotherapy*. New York: Liveright, 1950.

CHAPTER 5

Deviations in Psychoanalysis: II

In this chapter we shall consider what might be called the latter-day deviants in the psychoanalytic movement. We shall deal with the theories and practices of four so-called "dynamic-cultural" psychoanalysts (Horney, Sullivan, Fromm, and Anderson), with modifications of psychoanalysis in the direction of briefer and more directive treatment (psychoanalytically oriented psychotherapies), and with a new philosophical orientation which has developed especially among theoretical European analysts (existential analysis). The latter two developments will be treated quite briefly because their practical effects on psychotherapy can be briefly and simply stated. The systems of Horney, Fromm, and Anderson will also be handled rather summarily not only because much of their published work which bears directly on psychotherapy can be succinctly expressed, but also because the popularly written works of all three are readily available.

The bulk of this chapter treats the personality theory and psychotherapeutic system of Harry Stack Sullivan. The devotion of the major portion of our space to Sullivan has three justifications: (1) his contributions were brought to a higher and more complicated level of conceptualization than those of the other dynamic-culturalists and seem to be of more widespread and deeper influence in the growing, changing field of psychotherapy; (2) his publications (for the most part posthumous and for the most part transcribed from recordings of his lectures) are not easily understood and digested by the layman; and (3) his work, for both of the foregoing reasons, resists extreme condensation.

A. HORNEY

Karen Horney was trained as a Freudian analyst in Germany and came to the United States in the early 1930's. She soon made a break with the classical psychoanalytic movement and founded a separate association and training institute, which she headed until her death in 1952. Although she considered her theories "corrective" of Freud, rather than a completely new approach, she rejected both his instinct theory and his structural theory of the mind (id, ego, superego).

The underlying determining principle for human behavior, according to Horney, is not Freud's instincts of sex and aggression, but the need for security. When the security of the child in relation to his parents reaches unmanageable proportions, he develops an all-pervasive feeling of the world as a hostile and dangerous place. This feeling is what Horney calls basic anxiety.

The anxious person develops various strategies by which to cope with his feelings of isolation and helplessness. Any one of these strategies may assume the character of a drive or need in the dynamics of the personality. They are irrational (hence neurotic) attempts to find the solution for the problems of disturbed human relationships. Horney speaks of ten such neurotic needs: (1) for affection and approval, (2) for a "partner" who will take over one's life, (3) for restriction of life with narrow borders, (4) for power, (5) for exploitation of others, (6) for prestige, (7) for personal admiration, (8) for personal achievement, (9) for self-sufficiency and independence, and (10) for perfection and unassailability. These ten needs are the sources from which inner conflicts develop. Or, stated somewhat more pointedly, inner conflicts result from the interplay of these neurotic needs. A vicious circle is set up. If, for example, the neurotic asserts his need to be independent, he aggravates his unsatisfied need to be loved and admired.

These ten neurotic needs, Horney felt, fall under three general headings: moving toward people, moving away from people, and moving against people. The normal person also has some degree of conflict among these three broad categories of needs, but achieves a considerable degree of balance and integration among them. The neurotic person, however, tends to create an idealized image of himself in which the contradictory trends presumably disappear (but are actually only repressed).

The neurotic's idealized self-image, according to Horney, is not merely a false belief in his value and significance, but a kind of monster which comes increasingly to usurp his best energies and thus his ability to realize his potentialities. The neurotic becomes bent on actualizing his idealized self, which entails not only a search for worldly glory, but also a dedication to a tyrannical inner system whereby he tries to mold himself into a godlike being. He makes special claims on the world for attention, consideration, and deference, on the one hand, and develops, on the other hand, an unrealistic pride (as distinguished from a healthy self-confidence) which prevents him from doing the things that might achieve for him some of the worldly glory he feels to be his right.

The heart of neurosis, then, as Horney conceived it, is a disturbance in the patient's relation to self and to others. The godlike being (that is, the idealized self-image) is bound to hate the person's actual being (what Horney called the *actual self*). Along with the concepts of the idealized self (the neurotic, prideful, glory-seeking aspects of the personality) and the actual self (the whole personality of the individual as it actually exists at any point in time), Horney spoke of the "real self." By the latter she meant the central inner force of the individual which she believed to be the source of free, healthy development of personality potential. The real self is what the actual self can become by the therapeutic overthrow of the idealized self. The central inner conflict of the neurotic, as Horney saw it, is a battle between the constructive forces of the real self and the obstructive force of the pride system, between healthy growth and the neurotic drive to prove in actuality the perfections of the idealized self.

Horney's main idea of therapy, therefore, became that of giving the disturbed individual help in fighting the idealized self-image (including all the neurotic needs tied in with this image), realistically facing the actual self (seeing himself as he now is), and releasing the real self (that is, replacing the obstructive forces of pride with healthy growth). The idealized image offers a major stumbling block in therapy, according to Horney, because the recognition of these as neurotic trends means for the patient a collapse of what he perceives to be his integrity as a person. Yet it is only by putting the patient therapeutically through this "disillusioning process" and thus weakening the obstructive forces, the therapist helps the patient to release the constructive forces of the real self for healthy growth.

Like some of the earlier psychoanalytic dissidents, Horney believed in a more directive and active therapeutic role for the analyst than did Freud and his classical followers. She felt that the various strategies in relation to neurotic needs, the neurotic trends, the glory-seekings and pride systems of the idealized self-image, should be interpreted to the patient.

B. SULLIVAN

As a system builder in psychotherapy, Harry Stack Sullivan is probably second only to Freud. Sullivan in his later years (he died in 1949) seemed to feel some strong urge to present a well-rounded theory of human behavior. Sullivan was sensitive, too, about being considered a mere deviant from Freudian psychoanalytic theory and seems at times to use neologisms and circuitous explanations in order to appear independent of Freud. (It may be true, however, that he felt he thus avoided ambiguities and misconceptions.) The chief influences on Sullivan, as a matter of fact, were not so much Freud as the psychobiologic psychotherapy of Adolf Meyer (see Chapter 8), the broad humanistic psychiatric teachings of William Alanson White, and his own experience as a clinical psychiatrist.

Sullivan showed a remarkable understanding of not only what goes on inside people, but also what takes place between people as they relate to one another. His major thesis was that the primary concern of psychiatry is the study of interpersonal relations.

Sullivan's conception of interpersonal relations included more than what goes on between two or more people in interaction. He also referred to the relationships a person may have with imaginary people (such as one's "dream girl" or "the man who will some day take me away from all this"), with illusory or fantastic personifications (such as the kind of idealization of one's childhood sweetheart that Dante conjured up with Beatrice; or an illusion of some such personified entity as "the government," with which one interacts).

Whenever, in an interpersonal situation, persons react to a personification existing at least partly in fantasy, what Sullivan called *parataxic distortion* occurs. This would include what the Freudians refer to as transference (displacement of early childhood attitudes toward a significant person onto the therapist), but is more broadly any attitude toward another person based on fantasy or on identification of that person with other figures. Thus, in Sullivan's terms, the patient is interacting with a personification of this childhood person, not realistically with the therapist, and one of the main purposes of therapy, as Sullivan saw it, was to help the patient to see the parataxic distortions which kept him from making secure and satisfying interpersonal relationships.

Sullivan divided the purposes or goals of human behavior into two interrelated classes: the pursuit of satisfactions and the pursuit of security. Satisfactions, as he used the term, refers to biological needs, including sleep and rest, sex fulfillment, food and drink, and physical closeness to other human animals. Security, on the other hand, was used by Sullivan to refer to a state of well-being, of belonging, of being accepted. Most psychological problems, he pointed out, arise in relation to the pursuit of security. At times a society will interfere seriously with the biological satisfactions (most often sex in our society), but generally things go wrong in the formation or in the carrying out of security operations. When the individual has a state of "good feeling," or euphoria, security has been achieved. When he has a loss of euphoria, uneasiness, anxiety, his pursuit of security has been (at least temporarily) unsuccessful.

The process of becoming a human being is, in Sullivanian terms, the process of socialization. From birth onward values of the culture (conveyed in attitudes of persons around him) are transmitted to the child. The child begins to experience feelings of euphoria or security whenever he behaves "correctly" according to the values held by his parents or parent-substitutes and feelings of insecurity whenever he behaves "incorrectly."

Before the infant is even aware of himself as something separate from his surroundings, some of the attitudes of the person Sullivan called "the mothering one" are conveyed to him through "empathy." While Sullivan was not too explicit about what he meant by the term "empathy," he apparently viewed it as a biologically derived means of emotional communication. For example, if the mothering one feels anxiety for any reason around feeding time, this anxiety is somehow communicated to the infant. By such "emotional contagion and communion" from the mothering one, Sullivan thought, the infant first acquired his own feelings of anxiety.

Sullivan considered anxiety a potent, but restrictive, force in the formation of the self. As a result of early experiences of anxiety, human beings become, to varying degrees, "inferior caricatures of what they might have been." (In Horney's terms, the actual self falls far short of the real self.) The existence of large undeveloped areas of personality is most obvious in the highly disturbed, and Sullivan's therapeutic work was directed mainly toward people with severe mental disorders, especially schizophrenics. Much of Sullivan's therapeutic activity was focused on the parataxic distortions which had been produced by, and served to perpetuate, anxiety states in the patient. As a result of his experience of anxiety in childhood, the disturbed person has a highly distorted picture of himself and his relationships with others (these are his parataxic distortions). Such pictures were developed unthinkingly just to remove or reduce anxiety. Because the individual feels deeply, but irrationally, that they continue to provide him the means of avoiding anxiety, they are maintained until the disturbed person can be helped by the therapist to work through these distorted concepts and develop more rational, realistic concepts.

If, in the course of growing up, an individual is fortunate enough to have sound interpersonal relations with his peer group, especially with a close chum in adolescence, he may get some of his parataxic distortions corrected. Life itself, in other words, and not only psychotherapy, can provide corrective experiences. However specifically achieved, such correction, accomplished by comparing one's thoughts and feelings with others, Sullivan called "consensual validation."

In the process of the development of the self, the infant, Sullivan postulated, gradually evolves three personifications of "me": "good me," "bad me," and "not me." The "good me" is an organization of the experiences of the security feelings. The "bad me" is an organization of the experiences related to anxiety states. The "not me" seems to originate from "primitive anxiety," what Sullivan called the "uncanny" experiences of horror, dread, awe, and loathing in infancy. The "not me" feelings generally reveal themselves only in psychotic episodes and in night terrors and nightmares.

If experiences which bring security feelings predominate in the life of the developing child, the "good me" tends essentially to represent his conception of his self. If he meets an unusual number of unfortunate anxiety-producing experiences, he identifies primarily with the "bad me." Put differently, the child evaluates himself in terms of the reactions toward him he sees in the significant persons around him. If the parents and other significant persons show him a great deal of love, respect, and tenderness, he grows up with a conception of himself as worthy of love and esteem (the "good me" prevails). If the attitudes of the significant persons are largely negative, the child grows up without self-love and self-esteem (the "bad me" reigns).

The term "dynamism" is important in Sullivan's system. He defined dynamism as "the relatively enduring pattern of energy transformations which recurrently characterize the organism in its duration as a living organism." It refers to a kind of package of processes—the ways in which energy is organized and channeled in the organism. Sullivan applied the term dynamism to the whole emerging self, but also to part-systems within the developing self-dynamism. The lust dynamism, for example, was analyzed by Sullivan into the following components: (1) a psychobiological integrating apparatus, (2) a system of zones of interaction, (3) a pattern of covert and overt symbolic events, and (4) a system of integrating tendencies.

The emergent self-dynamism determines the aspects of the total available experience that will be utilized and integrated by the individual at any point in his life. Sullivan used the term "selective inattention" for the method used by the self-dynamism to control focal awareness so that what does not make sense in terms of the particular individual's self organization needs to get no attention. Particularly during the juvenile era, when the individual has an opportunity to test his ideas and values with his contemporaries (consensual validation), his self-dynamism develops the guide values for those things which are and those which are not worthy of attention (Sullivan's designation of "the juvenile era" will be given below).

Some things are so threatening to the security of the self, however, that they simply cannot be faced by the individual. The aspects of the individual's experience that lead to acute anxiety tend to be excluded from his awareness before they can bring their attendant anxiety. This mental process is essentially what the Freudians refer to as repression and is what Sullivan called *dissociation.*

Like Freud, Sullivan was interested in the developmental history of the individual and presented his conception of stages. Sullivan's stages of development are not, however, based on the emerging biological needs of the individual, but are characteristically related to the social patterns and the interpersonal relations, of the individual at various points in life. Sullivan's stages of development follow:

1. *Infancy*—from a few minutes after birth to the appearance of articulate speech. 2. *Childhood*—from the appearance of the ability to speak articulately to the appearance of a need for playmates. 3. *Juvenile era*—from the beginning of association with companions until the emergence of a need for an intimate relationship with another person of comparable status. 4. *Preadolescence*—the chum period, which ends with the eruption of genital sexuality and a change of strong interest from a person of one's own sex to a person of the other sex. 5. *Early adolescence*—the patterning of some type of performance which satisfied one's genital drives. 6. *Late adolescence*—from the achievement of such a lust-satisfying pattern until one is able to establish a love relationship in which the other person is nearly as significant as one's self (at which point one enters adulthood).

In discussing the human organism and its interpersonal relations at various stages of development, Sullivan emphasized the child's capacity to deal with various types of symbolization in his reactions to his environment. The goals of human behavior remain the same throughout all the stages: the pursuit of satisfactions (fulfilling biological needs) and the pursuit of security (avoidance of anxiety and attainment of "good feeling"). The means to the goals, however, the methods of pursuing the two basic purposes, depend on the individual's growing capacities in the various stages to understand and manipulate symbols in his social environment.

Sullivan typed people according to their most prevalent interpersonal attitudes. Although he did not offer the list as comprehensive, he said that he had observed ten syndromes, as follows: (1) nonintegrative: the so-called psychopathic personality (the chronic liar, thief, cheat, etc., who seems to lack any strong social feelings); (2) self-absorbed: a person characterized by fantastic, wishful thinking; (3) incorrigible: an individual who is hostile and forbidding toward all people except those whom he can regard as his inferiors (toward whom he has a kind, benevolent attitude); (4) negativistic: people who have given up hope of getting love and approval from others and who have therefore come to settle for attention; (5) the stammerer; (6) the ambition-ridden personality; (7) asocial: the detached, lonely people; (8) inadequate: the clinging-vine type; (9) homosexual (Sullivan considered homosexuality, like the other nine syndromes, a type of adjustment to anxiety and not a problem in itself); (10) chronic adolescent: the person who perpetually pursues, but never finds, the ideal in life.

Most of Sullivan's knowledge of personality was derived empirically from work with schizophrenics and obsessional cases. He learned early that the method of free association did not work well with these patients. Failure of other techniques he tried also led him to concentrate his attention on the communication process and the forces that aid and impede the transmission of meaning between people. In the course of his study Sullivan learned how important are the therapist's own attitudes, ideas, and actions in the therapeutic relationship. Thus derived Sullivan's emphasis on psychiatry as the study of interpersonal relations and on the therapist as a *participant* observer.

Just as the Freudians look for the origin of presenting symptoms in the repressed infantile unconscious of the patient, Sullivanians look for the source of characteristic syndromes in childhood experiences which have brought about massive dissociation in the patient. Sullivan apparently felt that for the patient to realize that his underlying anxieties and hostilities are understandable reactions to childhood hardship and confusion is of considerable assistance in facing the current consequences of such socialization. Unlike Freud (and more like Stekel and Adler), Sullivan felt that the therapist and patient needed to follow up such insight with a *direct attack* upon the old dissociations in order to break them down. Sullivan tried to maintain a back-and-forth movement in therapy between the analysis of the parataxic distortions revealed in the interpersonal relations of patient and therapist, of past situations as the source of these distortions and as a means of opening up dissociated reactions, and of the current life of the patient outside the therapeutic relationship.

For the particular kind of interpersonal relations that take place between the patient and the therapist, Sullivan used the term "psychiatric interview." He divided the interview into four stages: (1) the formal inception, (2) reconnaissance, (3) detailed inquiry, and (4) the termination.

In the inception, Sullivan stated, the interviewer should maintain mainly an attitude of quiet observation, during which he tries to understand the nature of the patient's problems. Sullivan stressed that the therapist should be alert not only to what the patient said, but how he said it (rate of speech, intonations, changes in volume, bodily position, facial expression, etc.). Although the therapist's main job at inception is quiet observation, Sullivan warned that he should not, even in the first interview, carry this role to the point where the patient feels he is simply being observed. The therapist should remember that he is an expert in interpersonal relations, and the patient should feel from the very first interview that he is learning something which will benefit him.

What Sullivan termed reconnaissance is the part in therapy where the therapist collects, by intensive interrogation, a great deal of biographical information about the patient. Although he advocated flexibility in the therapist's approach, he felt irrelevant and trivial matters should be ruled out.

As he moves into the third stage of the interviewing process (detailed inquiry), the therapist should, according to Sullivan, have several varying hypotheses to test out regarding the nature and source of the patient's difficulties. The therapist should realize that there is a constant two-way flow of ideas and feelings between the patient and therapist. Whenever communication becomes blocked, the therapist should ask himself what he has done to increase anxiety in the patient. The therapist needs to be constantly alert to his own attitudes and to control them in the interest of optimum communication.

Sullivan believed that the therapist should bring about a decisive and directive termination of the therapy. The therapist should summarize what he and the patient have learned about the patient and his (the patient's) interpersonal relations and should predict the probable effects of the patient's changed attitudes on his future interpersonal relations.

C. FROMM

Erich Fromm was trained as a psychologist, sociologist, and psychoanalyst in Europe before coming to the United States in 1933. Since his arrival in this country, he has had a great deal of influence on not only other psychoanalysts, but also on psychologists, sociologists, philosophers, religionists, and the general public. He has made no attempt, however, to develop a separate system of psychotherapy. He draws freely upon the concepts of all schools of psychoanalysis, including the Freudian (within which he had his original training), and he criticizes Freud and other analytic theorists only on points where he feels they have made either serious omissions or overemphases. Fromm nevertheless is most closely identified with the dynamic cultural points of view of Sullivan and Horney.

The essential theme of Fromm's writing is man's need to find meaning in his lonely, individuated life. Fromm holds that man can use his unique individual freedom to unite himself with his fellow men in a spirit of loving productiveness to achieve self-fulfillment and to develop a better society, or he can retreat from freedom by submitting himself to the bondage of an authoritarian society.

More specifically than either Horney or Sullivan, Fromm has tried to understand the interrelationships between the individual's psychic forces and the particular society in which he lives. Practically none of his interesting and, at times, profound analysis of these psychological and sociological interrelationships bear *directly* upon either the theories or techniques of psychotherapy. It is not contended that many of his significant historical and socioeconomic formulations, as well as his examination of the nature of individual dynamics, are not applicable to psychotherapy. It is simply stated that, for the most part, such applications have not been made (at least in writing) by Fromm or by anyone who holds to his formulations. It is quite probable, however, that through his stimulating effect on other therapists, through his challenging appeal to readers to overthrow their constricting conformity to irrational authority, and through his functioning as a teacher and therapist, Fromm has had as important an effect on the developing field of psychotherapy as any contemporary.

D. ANDERSON

A psychiatrist of the dynamic-cultural school who has apparently not yet developed a following among therapists, but whose theories have been presented to the public in nontechnical form, is Camilla Anderson. Her point of view does not seem to differ markedly from those of Sullivan, Horney, and Fromm (especially the latter). Trained in classical psychoanalytic techniques and theories, she arrived at her outlook, however, largely independently of the other dynamic-culturalists. We shall not repeat those aspects of her theories which are similar to those we have already considered. Her unique emphasis seems to be that of helping the individual to free himself from all morally judgmental attitudes and to replace them with critical conceptual judgments and realistic appraisals. Pride and guilt are two sides of the neurotic coin, as conceived by Anderson, and the patient needs to be helped to free himself of both in order to function in a practical and satisfying way in his social relationships. Psychotherapy is the process of becoming reality-oriented in place of moral-value-oriented. The therapist's job is to aid the patient in the process of getting acquainted with his own wants, feelings, capacities, and limitations, and then to evaluate the ways to improve his functioning in criticallv practical rather than moralistic terms.

E. PSYCHOANALYTICALLY ORIENTED PSYCHOTHERAPIES

With the possible exception of Ferenczi (who avoided an open break with Freud on theoretical grounds), all of the deviations from Freudian psychoanalysis we have considered thus far have not only included some alterations in the techniques recommended by Freud, but even more significant variations in theory. The psychoanalysts whose work we shall briefly consider in this section have held rather steadfastly to Freudian theory, but have experimented freely outside the classical psychoanalytic techniques. Probably a majority of psychoanalysts in the United States today have privately experimented with non-Freudian techniques, but relatively few have espoused such variations in public and professional forums. The four most widely known challengers of classical psychoanalytic techniques are (1) Alexander, French, and some other members of the Chicago Institute for Psychoanalysis; (2) Felix Deutsch and his system of "sector therapy"; (3) Benjamin Karpman and what he has called "objective psychotherapy"; and (4) John Rosen and his method of "direct analysis."

Alexander and his followers have attempted probably more than any other psychoanalytic group to subject their procedures to both critical examination and actual scientific experimentation. One of the main technical recommendations to emerge from these studies was the desirability at times to reduce and to interrupt therapeutic contacts with the patient. Interpretations, Alexander found, were often insufficient to counteract regressive dependency tendencies on the part of many patients. Such tendencies were not only combatted by properly-timed reduction of the frequency of interviews and interruptions in the therapy ("vacations" from the therapist during which some of the new insights can be "digested" and incorporated into the patient's behavior patterns), but also by encouraging the patient to undertake new life experiences outside therapy designed to increase his self-confidence.

The Chicago group believes that an intensely anxious individual may still need to be seen daily, especially during periods of great stress, but that less acutely anxious patients may progress quite well on three, two, or even one visit per week. In their experimentation with and without the couch in analysis, these investigators came to feel that it may be beneficial for shy, timid, guilt-ridden patients, but is likely to be a formidable obstacle to the progress in therapy of a hostile patient who cannot give way to his passive needs. The group's stress is on the desirability of having a plan of treatment that is modified as new facts emerge about the patient's personality and the problems he has to solve in his actual life conditions.

In addition to the points we have already mentioned, the Chicago group's technical flexibility includes occasional substitution of direct interviewing for free association, the offering to the patient of advice and suggestions about certain aspects of his life adjustment problems, and the utilization of life experiences that occur in order to advance certain treatment procedures. Greater emphasis is placed on the relationship between the therapist and patient rather than strictly on the transference, but positive transference is encouraged to establish rapport and enhance therapeutic progress and negative transference is analyzed when it blocks therapeutic progress. Stress is also given to the utilization of corrective emotional experiences which occur both in therapy and in the concurrent real life situations of the patient.

The "sector therapy" of Felix Deutsch is based considerably on the patient's associations to key words obtained from his autobiographical social history. While Deutsch does not feel that psychoanalytic treatment can be shortened in order to achieve extensive reconstructive goals, he believes limited goals can be achieved in the analytic interview by his technique of focusing on symptoms and conflicts which the patient's own key words and phrases have revealed. These key words and phrases will usually stimulate free associations in the patient. Deutsch advocates interrupting such free associations, however, when they veer away from the emotionally important material and then guiding the patient back to his key words and phrases. By this method, according to Deutsch, symptoms of present problems of the patient can be linked with underlying conflicts. Present associative chains of the patient are broken up by the therapist's confrontations, and new ones are formed. The patient's ego is thus helped to change its defensive attitudes and to discriminate present realities from past experiences.

In a somewhat related technique, Benjamin Karpman asks the patient, after a few preliminary interviews, to answer a series of questions taken from his own autobiography or from data otherwise secured by the therapist. Three separate series of questions are usually presented and, when written answers to these questions have been received, the therapist prepares a typed memorandum for the patient. Reading material may be given the patient regarding subjects related to his problems, and the patient's reactions in writing are also here requested. Dreams may also be written by the patient, and interpretations returned in writing by the therapist. Brief interviews are also held several times a week with the patient, but a close relationship between therapist and patient is avoided. At termination, a final memorandum as a whole is given to the patient. Karpman feels that this "objective psychotherapy," while more superficial than classical psychoanalysis, is well adapted to institutionalized patients and to persons with mild to moderate emotional disturbances.

Another psychiatrist, John Rosen, has adapted psychoanalytic techniques to his work with deteriorated psychotics. He has termed his procedures "direct analysis," and they consist of his efforts to enter directly into the symbolic worlds of the patients. Rosen takes at different times a series of roles symbolic of the people feared by his patients as expressed in their delusions and hallucinations. Working with excited catatonic, paranoid, and hebephrenic patients, Rosen tries to train his patients to feel that these feared people are now friendly and love the patients. This he demonstrates by helping the patients to do the things that the "voices" have frightened them away from doing previously. Interpretations coupled with strong positive transference and with the therapist's participation in the patient's world of fantasy have profound constructive effects, according to Rosen. He feels that in the treatment of schizophrenics the countertransference must be similar to the feelings that a good parent would have for a highly disturbed child. He contends that the therapist must identify with the unhappy patient in such a way that, like the good parent, he is disturbed by his unhappiness and cannot rest until the patient (child) is again at peace. While Rosen feels that the therapist must make up for the tremendous deficit of love which the patient has experienced in his early life, he does not shrink from vigorous physical contact should he feel, for example, that direct restraint is indicated in order to command the patient's attention or direct the stream of his thought. Although claimed cures have been spectacular, later reports and independent studies indicate considerable relapse.

F. EXISTENTIAL ANALYSIS

Another development of psychoanalysis has been its union with a form of European metaphysics called existential philosophy, and the resulting mixture has been appropriately termed existential analysis.

While the movement has achieved considerable support in Europe and parts of Asia, it has made little headway in the United States. Enough American interest is gradually developing, however, especially among analysts of the William Alanson White Institute and the Washington School of Psychiatry, to justify our giving existential analysis some brief attention.

Perhaps the foremost contemporary exponents of the existential philosophy are Martin Heidegger, Martin Buber, and Jean Paul Sartre. Various factors, including his extreme nihilism, have tended to exclude much of Sartre's point of view from consideration by psychoanalysts. Buber and Heidegger have been the most influential in the psychoanalytic movement. Of the European analysts who have applied the existential point of view to their therapeutic work, Medard Boss, Viktor Frankl, and Ludwig Binswanger are the best known. They follow the point of view of Heidegger.

Existential philosophy represents a European trend away from positivism, functionalism, instrumentalism, pragmatism, and operationalism—all of which tend to be close to the center of the value system of the scientist and of many American therapists. This is one reason for the lack of popularity of existential analysis in this country. Another reason is that existentialism is a philosophy of crisis, and the American scene does not yet reflect the European atmosphere of crisis. In an environment of desperation, man, as the existentialists see him, is striving for his forgotten power to *be;* man's plight is one of despairing for his *spontaneous existence.*

Existential analysts, then, emphasize the importance of the individual's values and goals and direct their attention toward understanding his personal world—his world of values. Their central contention seems to be that other therapists fail to formulate in explicit terms their understanding of the general nature and specific values of man and are therefore guided by hidden philosophical presuppositions which block their understanding of the patient. By analyzing the "meaning-structures" of each patient's personal world of values and by stripping themselves of preconceived notions about the nature and values of man, the existential analysts claim that they have discovered that the essential nature is a basic kind of being or "be-ness" and that the outstanding human value is a human unity, a being-together-in-the-world.

Although his terminology is at points different (and both the intellectual and emotional meanings of the German terms often defy translation into English), Viktor Frankl seems to be striving in the same general direction with his application of existentialism. Frankl emphasizes what he calls the "existential neurosis," which derives from the individual's inability to see meaning in life. Therapy consists largely in helping the patient to find an "authentic existential modality." The task of what Frankl calls "logotherapy" is to reveal the flaws in the patient's world-view (system of values) and to help him to achieve a readjustment of that view.

What does such understanding of the nature and values of man bring to the therapist? It does not, for the most part, lead him to depart from whatever psychoanalytic or psychotherapeutic procedures to which he previously adhered. It will, however, the existentialists assert, greatly change the attitude with which the therapist uses these tools in relating to the patient. If the therapist really understands that man is fundamentally a world-unfolding, world-opening being, he will have a kind of reverent love toward each such human being he encounters as a patient. He will see the patient with his personal world of values in terms of human existence (the be-ness) and the major value of human unity. The therapist will function himself and will try to aid his patient to function with the realization that man's intrinsic task is so to exist that he may help his fellow men most effectively to develop. The therapist will be aided, the existentialists postulate, to stand on the same place with his patients, the plane of common existence. He will relate to the patient as an existential partner in analyzing a reality of a present which is altogether continuous with the past and bears within it the possibilities of a future.

The foundation of the curative process in psychotherapy, according to this point of view, is the fundamental being-togetherness of therapist and patient. From the first encounter of patient and therapist, the latter, if existentially attuned, is together with his patient's way of existing (what other therapists have called "empathy" or "empathic understanding"). Also from the very first, the patient begins to partake of the therapist's way of living. Gradually as the sick patient, feeling understood and cared for by the therapist, gets the courage to emulate increasingly the therapist's healthy mode of existence and thus moves on to health himself by daring to be his own true self.

This, briefly, is the somewhat "spiritual" contribution of existential analysis. It offers no new techniques as such, and its theoretical contributions seem to lie mainly in the area of emphasis of certain values already recognized (albeit perhaps insufficiently practiced) by other psychotherapists.

Summary

The systems of four recent psychoanalytic deviants, the dynamic culturalists, have been reviewed in this chapter. We have also briefly considered psychoanalysts who have varied more in techniques than in theory under the heading of "psychoanalytically oriented psychotherapies." Our final section dealt with existential analysis.

The first of the dynamic culturalists, Karen Horney, considered the underlying determining principle of human behavior to be the need for security. When this need goes unfulfilled, the individual develops basic anxiety. The neurotic individual develops ten different kinds of strategies for handling anxiety, and these strategies themselves come to constitute neurotic needs. There are three characteristic patterns into which these needs fall, and the individual comes to structure his characteristic patterns into what Horney called his idealized self-image. Psychotherapy, in Horney's terms, becomes largely a process of helping the patient to fight his idealized self-image (including all the neurotic needs tied in with this image), to see himself as he actually is, and to replace the obstructive forces of his neurotic pride with healthy growth, thus releasing his real self.

Harry Stack Sullivan offered a much more complicated system of psychotherapy. He divided the purposes or goals of human behavior into two interrelated classes: the pursuit of satisfaction and the pursuit of security. The process of becoming a human being, Sullivan pointed out, is the process of socialization. The main object of the therapist's study should be the interpersonal relations of the patient: past, present (including those with the therapist), and future (for which the therapist must help him realistically prepare himself).

Anxiety, parataxic distortion, selective inattention, dissociation, dynamism, stages of development, and characteristic syndromes are key concepts of Sullivan's which are considered in this chapter, but which cannot be briefly summarized. Sullivan also made some original contributions to therapeutic techniques, which he developed under the heading of "the psychiatric interview."

Erich Fromm, the third dynamic culturalist, has made many important theoretical contributions to the understanding of the individual and his society, few of which, however, have dealt directly with psychotherapy. Fromm's essential theme is man's need to find meaning in his lonely, individuated life, which need he can fulfill only by uniting himself in a spirit of loving productiveness with his fellow men. Only in this way will man, according to Fromm, achieve self-fulfillment and develop a better society.

Camilla Anderson, who has independently developed a dynamic-cultural system that in many ways resembles those of Horney and Fromm, has made an original emphasis on man's need to free himself of all moral judgments and to substitute critical conceptual judgments and realistic appraisals.

The psychoanalytically oriented psychotherapists have largely confined themselves to the development of techniques which will bring greater speed and efficiency to the treatment of individuals who do not seem to need classical psychoanalysis and (in the case of Rosen) to the treatment of psychotics.

The central contention of existential analysis is that therapists fail to formulate in explicit terms their understanding of the general nature and goal of man and are therefore misled by hidden philosophical presuppositions. By stripping themselves of preconceived notions about the nature and goal of man, the existentialists hold, they have discovered that the essential nature is a basic kind of "be-ness" and the goal is a human unity, a being-togetherness. With attitudes derived from this understanding, the existential analyst feels he can be more helpful to his patient.

Selected Readings

Alexander, Franz, *Psychoanalysis and Psychotherapy*. New York: Norton, 1956.

Anderson, Camilla, *Beyond Freud*. New York: Harper, 1957.

Boss, Medard, *The Dream and Its Interpretation.* London: Rider, 1957.

Deutsch, Felix, and W. F. Murphy. *The Clinical Interview* (2 vols.). New York: Int. Univs., 1955.

Frankl, Viktor E., *The Doctor and the Soul; an Introduction to Logotherapy* (translated by Richard and Clara Winston). New York: Knopf, 1955.

Fromm, Erich, *Man for Himself.* New York: Rinehart, 1947.

Horney, Karen, *Neurosis and Human Growth.* New York: Norton, 1950.

May, Rollo, Ernest Angel, and Henri F. Ellenberger (Eds), *Existence: A New Dimension in Psychiatry and Psychology.* New York: Basic Books, 1958.

Rosen, John N., *Direct Analysis.* New York: Grune, 1953.

Sullivan, Harry Stack, *The Interpersonal Theory of Psychiatry.* New York: Norton, 1953.

———, *The Psychiatric Interview.* New York: Norton, 1954.

CHAPTER 6

Client-Centered Therapy

The first system of psychotherapy of widespread prominence that has its roots almost exclusively in American psychology (as distinguished from psychiatry, on the one hand, and European sources, on the other) is what was originally called nondirective counseling and more recently client-centered therapy. The originator and outstanding exponent of the system is Carl Rogers.

Rogers, with a background in liberal theology (Union Theological Seminary) and the progressive educational philosophy of John Dewey, as well as in clinical psychology (Teachers College, Columbia University), brought to his functioning as a counselor and psychotherapist a strong personal and professional predisposition toward permissiveness. In his clinical internship as a counselor, Rogers reacted negatively to what he saw as highly authoritarian psychotherapeutic procedures based on what he believed to be very speculative theories of human behavior (psychoanalysis). On his first full-time job as a counselor (Director, Rochester Guidance Center), Rogers was further influenced by his own experiences in treatment procedures, by his conferences with fellow staff members, and by the deviant psychoanalytic views of Otto Rank into an attitude of total permissiveness of counselor toward client. The permissive attitude rests on the proposition that the client has basic potentialities within him for growth and development. The main function of the therapist is to provide the atmosphere in which the client feels free to explore himself, to acquire deeper understanding of himself, and gradually to reorganize his perceptions of himself and the world about him.

Since leaving Rochester in 1940, Rogers has taught, as well as continuing in clinical and administrative work, at three major universities: Ohio State (1940-45), Chicago (1945-57), and Wisconsin (since 1957). During this period of time, he has trained many graduate students in his basic approach to psychotherapy, has sharpened and modified the details and rationale of client-centered therapy, has developed a theory of personality which corresponds to the therapy, has undertaken and stimulated in others much more research than any other "school" of therapy, and has likewise produced and stimulated others to produce a vast amount of professional literature on client-centered therapy and related topics.

There seem to be many reasons for the popularity of the Rogersian approach to therapy. One is that it fits snugly into the American democratic tradition. The client is treated as an equal, who has within him the power to "cure" himself, with no need to lean heavily on the wisdom of an authority or expert. Second, the client-centered philosophy of the person's potentiality for constructive change also fits in well with the optimistic aspect of American culture: the notion that if he meets the knock of opportunity with determination and good will, each individual can come to a good goal. Third, the client-centered way appeals to the young, insecure, inexperienced, prospective therapist as, at least superficially, the "easy way." It is unnecessary for the therapist to have any great knowledge of personality diagnosis or dynamics, and he takes no real responsibility for guidance of the disturbed client. He simply encourages the client to be more fully himself; he provides warmth and acceptance as the means whereby the client can achieve self-realization. Any permissive, warmly loving person can readily become a therapist via the client-centered system. Fourth, the method, at least in its early years, held promise of being a swifter route to personality change than did psychoanalysis. The fact that client-centered therapy no longer seems so brief may arise from the fact that more disturbed and more difficult patients have turned to client-centered therapists in recent years. And the fifth basic appeal of client-centered therapy has been its attraction for American psychologists who better understand its philosophical postulates, its respect for psychological research methods, and its lack of foreign terms and methods. This latter point has been partially negated, however, by the rapid diffusion (especially in the last decade) of the psychoanalytic point of view among clinical psychologists and the lingering behavioristic influence (especially in the psychology of learning) which views the phenomonological outlook of client-centered therapy as unscientific.

As we have indicated, Rogers' personality theory followed many years after his first developments of the client-centered techniques of therapy. The first written formulations of the therapy were presented in 1940, and the first full presentation of the personality theory did not appear until 1951. In our examination of client-centered therapy, however, we shall reverse the historical process. We shall follow the same procedure we have used in our consideration of other systems: first, a look at the conceptions of human behavior and, then, at the theories and techniques of therapy.

In developing his theory of personality, Rogers drew from the hypotheses of many psychologists (especially Goldstein, Snygg and Combs, Maslow, Angyal, Lecky) and, to some extent, the theories of Harry Stack Sullivan. Most essential in understanding the main theoretical conceptions of personality of Rogers and his associates is knowledge of what is called the phenomenological point of view. By this hypothesis, each person has a phenomenal field, which is a definition of events or phenomena as they appear to him. His behavior, according to the phenomenologists, is entirely determined by his field, and predictions of his behavior demand knowledge of that field.

If, for example, a clinician is trying to understand the behavior of a homosexual, he is wasting his time, according to the phenomenologists, to study statistics about homosexuality, studies of background factors in the development of homosexuals, theories of the etiology of homosexuality, etc. The valid source of information is the particular homosexual himself: how does *he* feel? How does life appear to *him?* What does *he* think about himself in relation to other people? Answers to such questions as these, Rogers and other phenomenologists say, are necessary really to understand the behavior of any individual and to predict how that individual will respond to future situations in or out of therapy.

A person's phenomenal field is limited. Only a small portion of experience can be held in focus at a given time. The phenomenal field becomes constantly restructured according to the person's need.

Freudians would say psychic content moves from the preconscious to the conscious mind, and Sullivanians speak of selective attention and inattention.

Those parts of the phenomenal field which the individual perceives as part or characteristic of himself are of particular importance in the determination of behavior, as understood by Rogers. These include the individual's physical self and his relationships with the cultural and physical worlds. Some of these things the individual considers relatively unimportant, and he leaves them rather vague and unattended. But those aspects of his phenomenal self which are highly differentiated and which he has defined as definite and relatively stable attributes of himself constitute the compelling aspects of his life and form his self-concept. Stated differently, the self-concept, or self-structure, is an organized configuration of perceptions of the self which are admissible to awareness.

It is difficult for a person not immersed in the Rogersian system to see clearly how the self-concept thusly defined differs markedly from Horney's idealized self-image. In psychological maladjustment, the two constructs would seem to be one and the same. Rogers speaks of psychological tension when the organism denies to awareness significant sensory and visceral experiences, which consequently are not organized in the self-concept. Hence, under those circumstances the Rogersian self-concept would strongly resemble the idealized self-image, which, the reader will remember, was a chief neurotic troublemaker in the Horneyian scheme of things. Presumably Horney's real self (and Fromm's true self) is approximated in Rogers' healthy individual's self-concept: when the concept of the self is such that all the sensory and visceral experiences of the organism are, or may be, assimilated on a symbolic level into a consistent relationship with the concept of the self.

When organic experiences and needs appear which have not been symbolized and which are inconsistent with the self, they are, in Rogers' terms, *disowned* by the individual. This comes close to Freud's idea of repression and Sullivan's notion of dissociation. The unconscious mind itself has no place in the Rogersian scheme of personality.

Rogers has pointed out that the values attached to experiences and those which are part of the self-concept may be either values directly experienced in the past by the organism or values taken over from others, but perceived in distorted fashion as if they had been experienced directly. The values that are taken over in this distorted fashion from others lead to confusion, unhappiness, and ineffectiveness. Such a person does not "know himself," for his organism (that is, his visceral and sensory perceptions) tells him one thing and his self-concept (the values he permits to enter his awareness) tells him another.

Within the framework of the phenomenological theory, the fundamental urge underlying all behavior is the need to preserve and enhance the phenomenal self. Any experience which is out of line with the structure of the self may be perceived as a threat, and the more threats there are, the more rigid the structure of the self to protect and maintain itself.

The reader will notice that Rogers has found it necessary to formulate two opposing systems, the organism and the self, which correspond roughly to Freud's id and ego and Jung's unconscious and conscious. The organism may have visceral and sensory experiences that the self does not let itself perceive because they are inconsistent with the self stucture.

With self preservation and enhancement the basic motivation of human behavior, the individual who is doing what seems (to us) obviously self-destructive acts must mistakenly perceive these acts as routes to self esteem. Therapy, then, consists of helping the individual to find ways of conceiving of himself that will free him of conflicts and which will allow him to function smoothly in his relationships with others. In client-centered therapy, which provides primarily an atmosphere free of any threat to the self-structure, the person can work out a harmonious integration of the self and the organism. In this environment, the individual may perceive, examine, and revise the self-structure to assimilate and include experiences formerly avoided as inconsistent with that structure. Thus assert the client-centered therapists.

The reality with which client and therapist deal, according to Rogers, is the reality of the present as perceived by the client. There is generally sufficient community of experience and sufficient overlapping of phenomenal fields, he believes, beween therapist and client to make possible a meaningful interchange of ideas and feelings. Past and future have relevance in the Rogersian system only insofar as they are conceptualized currently by the client or insofar as they constitute tensions that non-symbolically influence present behavior. Etiology, diagnosis, and prognosis are not matters that should occupy the client-centered therapist's mind. He should be concerning himself with the here and now of the client. Rogers feels that behavior is goal-directed, but needs and goals are part of the present, not the past or the future.

Rogers takes the position that the patient's reports are valid and reliable sources of information about his personality. The central feature of Rogers' conception of personality is the self-as-object, and it is assumed that consciously experienced self feelings can be communicated to the therapist. This position is in marked contrast to the psychoanalytic view that the patient's conscious impression of himself is highly invalid and unreliable as a source of information about true (unconscious) personality motivation. Rogers and his followers show little or no interest in dream interpretations, parapraxes, wit, or free association as routes to unconscious motivation; for, from the practical standpoint of its function in Rogersian therapy, unconscious motivation is non-existent.

As the client enters therapy, according to Rogers, he is likely to have a critical negative picture of himself. He has an idealized image of how he should be and is quite certain he miserably fails to measure up to this ideal. At first in therapy, he is apt to feel even more discouraged and self critical, but he begins to develop an awareness of quite contradictory attitudes toward himself. As he explores these attitudes, in the accepting and approving atmosphere supplied by the therapist, the patient begins more and more to accept himself as he is, including the contradictions. Both self-condemnation and self-approval begin to decrease, and objective observation of himself in action tends to be substituted. As these changes take place, the patient comes to feel himself a more real and unified person. His goals shift and become more achievable, and the discrepancy between his ideal self image and his perceptions of his real self become less and less. The patient's inner life thus becomes increasingly free of tension.

It is pertinent to note at this time that the Rogersian therapists have more objective or near-objective evidence to support their contentions about what happens in successful client-centered therapy than other schools of therapists can produce to support their contentions. Rogers and his followers have made more tape recordings and movies, conducted more research investigations, and opened their procedures more fully to inspection than any other system. It does not mean that their claims are all justified or that their principles and practices are sounder therapeutically than other systems. Our interpolation of comment about research at this point is simply intended to indicate in fairness that assertions regarding what happens to the client in client-centered therapy are not based simply on wishful thinking on the part of therapists of this persuasion. Our critical examination of the Rogersian system, along with all the others, will be reserved for Chapter 10.

The attitude taken by Rogers toward the role of diagnosis in therapy is rather unique. He feels that diagnosis is not only unnecessary, but unwise and detrimental. This attitude applies not only to all psychometric tests, but also to any stated opinions on the part of the therapist about the nature of the patient's problems. Rogers feels that the client may be ill-prepared to handle certain information diagnostically revealed to him and that diagnosis fosters the dependency of the client on the therapist as "the expert." Not only does diagnosis probably have a damaging effect on the attitudes of the client, according to Rogers, but likewise on the therapist. It is not the therapist, but the client who must make the decisions about changes in the client's behavior, and the less the therapist's attitudes are colored by a predetermined point of view the more he will be able to give the client the acceptance and positive regard that he (the client) needs to improve his mental health. Stated differently, the less the therapist thinks he knows as an expert, the less he will interfere with the client's freedom to develop the therapeutic situation to meet his own needs. And Rogers contends, as a final point, that the therapist has enough to do in simply understanding what it is that the client is trying to work through without trying simultaneously to formulate self queries designed to bring him (the therapist) to a point of diagnosis.

From some of the studies that have been made of the therapeutic process, the following characteristic activities of the client-centered therapist have emerged: (1) Strong, consistent effort to understand the client's content of speech and feelings conveyed by words, gestures, expressions, etc.; (2) an effort to communicate this understanding to the client by word or (more often) his general attitude of acceptance; (3) occasional presentation of a condensation or synthesis of expressed feelings; (4) occasional statement of the nature and limits of the therapeutic relationship, the expectancies of the situation, and the therapist's confidence in the ability of the client to handle his problems; (5) when question-answering and information-giving seem relevant to the client's working through of his problems, they are engaged in, but denied when they seem likely to increase the client's dependency; (6) while the therapist may interrupt the client to make sure he understands what the client is saying or feeling, he offers no interpretations other than those which seem to summarize what the client (not the therapist) is feeling; (7) likewise the client-centered therapist does not try to promote insight directly, or to give advice, praise, blame, or to teach or suggest programs of activities, or to ask questions or suggest areas of exploration.

While certain aspects of client-centered therapy are characteristic of most, but not all, of the systems discussed in this book, there is one issue on which client-centered therapy is different from all of the others. That one issue is the leaving of all responsibility for the course and direction of therapy to the client. The choice of topic of discussion, the finding of meanings, the speed or lack of speed with which the client faces certain problems in his life, the frequency and degree of digressions, the follow-up of what seems to be a significant area for exploration—all of these and comparable decisions are made by the client, not the therapist, in client-centered therapy.

When is an individual ready for therapy, in client-centered terms? It is when his organized self-structure no longer effectively meets the needs of the reality-situations in which he finds himself, or when he feels a significantly large cleavage between what he wants to be and what he is. Such a person, either vaguely or clearly feeling anxiety, enters client-centered therapy and, according to Rogers, experiences a kind of freedom which is decidedly new to him. While the patient has been in other situations where he was not directly attacked, he has never before had every aspect of self which he exposed equally accepted and valued. His belligerencies, uncertainties, perceptions of contradictions, discouragements are not challenged, belittled, or contradicted, but are accepted and valued. In this atmosphere of safety and acceptance, Rogers contends, the firm and defensive boundaries of self are relaxed, and the patient is able to consider objectively his contradictory perceptions and experiences and gradually assemble a new personality gestalt.

Client-centered therapy, Rogers says, is a process of disorganization and reorganization of the self. The new organization contains more accurate symbolization of a much wider range of sensory and visceral experience, a reconceptualized system of values based on the person's own feelings and experiences (in place of the old, largely borrowed, second-hand values). The painful dis- and reorganization can be made by the client mainly because his old contradictory attitudes are not only accepted by the therapist, but the new and difficult patterns as well. The client comes to introject the calm acceptance of the therapist and can handle the new and difficult reality perceptions necessary for the reorganization.

As the new self-structure becomes firmer and more clearly defined, it provides the client with a steadier guide for his actual behavior. Positive attitudes increasingly predominate over negative, and the client sees in himself more and more a pattern of behavior drawn from experience, rather than a pattern imposed upon experience. Because the value system is based more on actual experience, it feels more realistic and comfortable and in harmony with the perceived self. Ideals seem more achievable. Also overt behavior is more adjustive and socially more sound, because the assumptions on which it rests are more realistic.

While Rogers admits that some transference attitudes (usually mild, but occasionally strong) appear in client-centered therapy, he maintains that these attitudes do not develop into a transference relationship or a transference neurosis. This, he says, is because the client-centered therapist's reaction to transference is the same as to any other attitude of the client: he tries to understand and accept. Acceptance then leads to the recognition by the client that these feelings are within himself, not in the therapist. The impersonal and secure attitudes of the therapist soon lead the client to abandon a belief that the feelings displaced (transferred) to the therapist belong elsewhere than inside him, the client. Rogers hypothesizes that a transference relationship is most likely to occur when the client experiences the therapist as having a more effective understanding of his own self than he himself possesses, a situation that cannot develop in correctly operated client-centered therapy (because the therapist looks to the client as the true source of information about the client's self).

In the early development of his system of psychotherapy, Rogers set certain limitations regarding the sorts of persons who could be helped by the client-centered approach. These limitations referred to such matters as age, intelligence, freedom from family control, and absence of excessive instabilities. More recently he has expressed reluctance about setting arbitrary limits of effectiveness. Work with mentally defective and delinquent individuals has been negligible, but success has been obtained with some individuals in almost every other category of pathology, according to Rogers. Since the nature of client-centered therapy is such that harm is not likely to result to any individual not helped, Rogers contends, there is no reason to preclude experimenting with the technique with any type of patient. This is true, Rogers says, because of the lack of any pressure in the relationship: the person draws back from subjects too upsetting or dangerous to face.

Quite recently, Rogers has addressed himself to the question of what psychological conditions are necessary and sufficient to bring about constructive personality change. By "constructive personality change" (he also uses the alternate phrase of "psychotherapeutic change"), he means an alteration of the personality structure of the individual in a direction of greater maturity, integration, and energy utilizable for effective living. The six necessary and sufficient conditions Rogers has presented are discussed in the following paragraphs.

He points out, first of all, that significant positive personality change does not occur except in a relationship. His first condition, then, is simply psychological contact: the awareness of both the client and the therapist of the presence of the other.

Rogers' second condition as necessary for psychotherapeutic change is that the client is in a stage of "incongruence." The term refers to a difference between the actual experience of the individual and his self picture. When the individual is even vaguely aware of such incongruence, he is anxious. When he is not aware, he is nevertheless vulnerable to the possibility of anxiety. A client in a state of incongruence, either anxious or vulnerable to anxiety, is, then, this second necessary condition.

The third necessary condition for a client's constructive personality change is that the therapist be congruent or integrated in the relationship. Rogers states that this means simply that the therapist must be freely, deeply, genuinely himself, with his actual experience accurately represented by his awareness of himself. This includes being himself in ways that are not therapeutically ideal. He may feel bored, for example, or preoccupied with his own problems, but so long as he does not deny these feelings to his own awareness, he meets Rogers' definition of functioning congruently.

Fourthly, it is necessary that the therapist experience unconditional positive regard for his client, according to Rogers. This means that the therapist must find himself experiencing a warm acceptance of each aspect of the client's experience as being a part of that client. The acceptance can be in no way conditional: it is caring for the client as a separate person, with full permission from the therapist to have his own feelings and experiences.

Rogers' fifth necessary condition is that the therapist must experience an empathic understanding of the client's awareness of his own experience and that he must try to communicate this empathic understanding to the client. The definition Rogers gives of empathic understanding is that of sensing the client's internal frame of reference as if it were his (the therapist's) own without the therapist's losing his own separate emotional existence. It is the ability of the therapist to sense the client's emotions without himself getting emotionally tied up in them. He comes, as Rogers puts it, to move around freely in the client's emotional world, and then to be able to communicate his understanding to the client (including things the client himself has only vaguely sensed).

It is, then, at least the minimally effective communication of both the therapist's empathic understanding and the therapist's unconditional positive regard that is Rogers' sixth and final necessary condition for constructive personality change. The client must perceive that the therapist empathizes and accepts or such attitudes do not exist in the relationship so far as the client is concerned (no matter how deeply the therapist may feel he is experiencing them). Stated differently, the therapist's behavior and words must be perceived by the client to add up to at least some degree of acceptance and understanding of him.

Rogers has unequivocally stated that if the foregoing six conditions are fulfilled, then effective psychotherapeutic results can be achieved. He feels that this is true regardless of the type of emotional disturbance presented by the client and dismisses contentions of other therapists that conditions vary as the therapist attempts to help neurotics, homosexuals, psychotics, etc.

Few, if any, therapists of whatever persuasion would deny that the conditions Rogers lists are desirable. Most would probably even agree that they are necessary. Few other than client-centered therapists, however, would join Rogers in believing that they are sufficient. Some direction out of the maze, following upon the establishment of empathy and positive regard, would be called for in many systems of psychotherapy.

One of the noteworthy omissions from Rogers' list of necessary and sufficient conditions for therapeutic personality change is any professional training or knowledge for the psychotherapist. Any person who gains experience in functioning as an integrated, or congruent, accepting, empathic person could meet Rogers' criteria of an effective therapist. Psychological, psychiatric, and medical knowledge would become not only irrelevant to effective operation as a therapist, but might even be severe handicaps (along the lines already mentioned earlier of making the therapist feel that he is an "expert" and inclined to engage in diagnosis).

The main merit of Rogers' formulations of the necessary and sufficient conditions for effective therapeutic personality change is that they are hypotheses that can be readily tested. Already research is under way to shed some light on the degree of truth that may be contained in these rather radical postulates.

The client-centered point of view has spread far beyond individual psychotherapy. Application of the basic approach has been made in education, play therapy, group therapy, industrial and business administration, various aspects of religious work, in the training of counselors and therapists, and elsewhere. With the exception of group therapy (the Rogersian approach to which is considered in Chapter 9), these applications are beyond the scope of our attention. They are mentioned to give the reader an idea of the extent and impact of what is essentially an ubiquitous development of an American philosophy: the individual who is, by love and acceptance and understanding, helped to become effectively the master of his own destiny.

How well does client-centered therapy work? Despite their unexcelled research, the Rogersians have not supplied us with satisfactory answers to this question. We know little about their successes compared with successes of other therapeutic systems. We know even less about their failures. To say that other schools of therapy have provided us with even less satisfactory answers regarding the effectiveness of their approaches is true enough. To say, further, that Rogers and his followers have challenged *all* psychotherapists to seek more factual proof of their contentions, to re-examine their theories and techniques in the full and open and objective light of science, is an even more pertinent truth regarding the future health and value of the whole field of psychotherapy. It is the very least tribute objectively earned by Carl Rogers and his client-centered psychotherapeutic system.

Summary

Client-centered psychotherapy is based on a phenomenological conception of human behavior. By this view, each person has a phenomenal field, which is a definition of events or phenomena as they appear to him. His behavior is determined by his field, and prediction of his behavior demands knowledge of that field.

Carl Rogers, chief proponent of client-centered therapy, has pointed out that values which become an integral part of the individual's phenomenal field may be derived either from direct experience or taken from others. The values which are taken over in a distorted fashion from others lead to confusion, unhappiness, and ineffectiveness. This type of person does not "know himself," for his organism tells him one thing and his self-concept tells him another. Such an incongruent individual, anxious or vulnerable, is a likely candidate for psychotherapy.

Client-centered therapy, according to Rogers, is a process of disorganization and reorganization of the self. The new organization contains more accurate symbolization of a much wider range of sensory and visceral experience, a reconceptualized system of values based on the person's own feelings and experiences. The painful dis- and reorganization can be made by the client mainly because his old contradictory attitudes are not only accepted by the therapist, but the new and difficult patterns as well. The client comes to introject the calm acceptance of the therapist and can handle the new and difficult reality perceptions necessary for the reorganization.

Rogers has postulated that psychotherapeutic personality change can be and will be effected when the following conditions are fulfilled: a psychological contact between therapist and client, a state of incongruence in the client, a state of congruence in the therapist, unconditional positive regard for and empathic understanding of the client by the therapist, and the client's perception of the therapist's positive regard for and empathic understanding of him. Diagnosis, professional knowledge, and other frequently emphasized characteristics of the therapist are not considered necessary by Rogers and may, indeed, according to him, be obstructive.

Whatever the degree of truth in the client-centered point of view, the empirical researches undertaken by the group and the challenge that this position has offered to other psychotherapeutic systems has been a healthful influence in the general field of psychotherapy.

Selected Readings

Rogers, Carl R., *Client-Centered Therapy*. Boston: Houghton, 1951.

———, *Counseling and Psychotherapy*. Boston: Houghton, 1942.

———, "The Necessary and Sufficient Conditions of Therapeutic Personality Change." *Journal of Consulting Psychology,* 1957, 21, 95-103.

———, and Rosalind F. Dymond (Eds), *Psychotherapy and Personality Change*. Chicago: U. of Chicago, 1954.

CHAPTER 7

A Variety of Systems: I

To this point we have considered psychoanalysis in its manifold variations and the relatively independent development of client-centered therapy. In the next two chapters, we turn our attention to eleven somewhat separate therapeutic developments, some of which are more deserving of the term "system" than others. All, however, have brought an emphasis in theory and/or technique that makes them of at least some significance in understanding the contemporary psychotherapeutic scene.

In this chapter, we shall deal with six systems of psychotherapy: psychobiologic therapy, Gestalt therapy, hypnotherapy, experiential therapy, conditioned-reflex therapy, and psychotherapy by reciprocal inhibition. Psychobiologic, Gestalt, and experiential therapies are systems that are integrative of a number of points of view, with original emphases within each. Hypnotherapy is a system which stresses the value of the particular technique of hypnosis in both short-term, re-educative and long-term, reconstructive therapy. Conditioned-reflex therapy and psychotherapy by reciprocal inhibition are radical departures from other therapeutic systems.

A. PSYCHOBIOLOGIC THERAPY

Adolf Meyer is a psychiatrist who tried to integrate all forms of psychotherapy and the various biological and medical approaches to treatment. Meyer did not discard psychoanalytic procedures, but tended to emphasize the environmental manipulative and supportive approaches. He also put much stress on the securing of complete medical and social histories. Meyer and his students developed a diagnostic classification system based not on diseases, but on "reaction types," or categories by predominant symptoms. The Meyerian system is generally referred to as "psychobiologic therapy" and its characteristic procedures are termed "distributive analysis and synthesis."

As already indicated, Meyer emphasized the importance of obtaining a clear and full understanding of the patient's own views of his problem, and to this end encouraged the extensive recordings of the interviews. Although the patient is encouraged to describe himself, his background, and current difficulties, the psychobiologist does not hesitate to furnish positive assistance whenever the patient indicates a need for help in giving a fully rounded picture of his situation.

The psychobiologist gives great importance to the patient's point of view in his clinical judgments, but he knows that emotional disturbances fall into familiar categories of symptom combinations. He therefore uses his knowledge of these categories in analyzing and synthesizing facts about the patient. The therapist of psychobiological orientation also knows that he himself has been influenced by his culture to accept certain mental patterns and so does not proceed under the illusion that he can be completely unbiased regarding the values held by the patient. Although the psychobiologist does not attempt to function as simply a mirror of the patient's values, he tries to be aware of his own biases and is careful not to inflict these on the patient.

The effort of psychotherapy, as viewed psychobiologically, is to achieve a synthesis of the views of the patient and therapist which will be the most effective and satisfying for the patient. The therapist needs to stress for both himself and the patient that the therapeutic activity is a joint search for a desirable resolution of the patient's problem and is not an "instruction" of the patient by the therapist: The therapist seeks to make sure that the way of life which is the outcome of this co-operative enterprise is indeed better for the patient than the one he had arrived at alone, prior to the therapy.

The chief disturbances of patients, as the psychobiologist sees them, are those which consist of compulsive habits and accompanying emotions derived from childhood experiences. These habits and concomitant emotional attitudes can be set off by both relevant and irrelevant stimuli, and the patient becomes a kind of prisoner of these irrational, childish patterns. The most destructive of these attitudes in the character formation of the individual are self-hate and self-disrespect. The kinds of character difficulties which develop from these self-attitudes can vary from timidity and feeling of inadequacy (which prevent realization of full personality potential) on through the extreme manifestations such as outward-directed hostility of the sociopathic and criminal personality types or to inward-directed hostility conditions, such as morbid fears, paranoid tendencies, and depressive states.

Since the psychobiologist tries to manage the treatment situation to accomplish the best possible collaboration between the particular patient and himself, he remains flexible and eclectic regarding techniques. Unlike adherents of some therapeutic systems, he does not place certain techniques above personality or situational factors. The Meyerian feels he must be ever ready to alter his methods from directive to nondirective, from suggestive to passively receptive, in accordance with the progress of the collaborative effort and in the light of his knowledge of the patient (derived both from the history and from the therapeutic situation).

The psychobiologist at times uses interpretation as one of his therapeutic tools. Meyer conceived of interpretation as the therapist's use of intellectualized concepts to promote the patient's understanding of the situation—hopefully not only in intellectual, but also in volitional and emotional, terms. Interpretation is offered, never forced, by the psychobiologist at a time that he thinks the patient is ready to use it and able to absorb it.

B. GESTALT THERAPY

The contributions of Gestalt psychology have been most notable in the study of perception. One attempt has been made, however, to apply it much more extensively to the whole area of psychotherapy. Three men, Frederick Perls, Ralph F. Hefferline, and Paul Goodman, are co-authors of this work (*Gestalt Therapy*. New York:

Julian Press, 1951). These writers believe that the Gestalt point of view is the natural and undistorted approach to the wholeness of life by human beings. The Gestaltists contend that in the course of his contact with our culture, the average person gets his integrity of thinking, feeling, and acting fragmented. Gestalt therapy is the effort to heal patients of their dualism of being, to redevelop the unitary outlook.

In proceeding with their Gestalt theories of psychotherapy, the authors draw on material from various other psychological and psychotherapeutic points of view (especially psychoanalytic), but feel that they bring new meaning to these selected materials by their differing synthesis.

The German word "Gestalt," the authors point out, lacks an exact English equivalent. Words which most closely approximate the German meaning are configuration, meaningful organized whole, structural relationship, and theme. The "Gestalt" is the meaningful organized whole of a figure and its background. The "ground" in Gestalt psychology is the context against which the element (the "figure") stands out.

The interplay of figure and ground becomes the focus of the Gestalt theory of personality and therapy as presented by Perls and his associates. The healthy person has a permanent, meaningful emerging and receding of figure and ground. Attention, interest, excitement, grace, concentration, and concern are characteristic of his figure/ground formation. Neurotics and psychotics, on the other hand, have either a rigidity (fixation) or a lack of figure formation (repression) as opposed to the healthy person's elasticity of emerging and receding figure and ground. A disturbed individual's figure/ground formation is characterized by confusion, boredom, compulsions, fixations, anxiety, and self-consciousness.

Perls and his co-authors stress that neither the understanding of the functions of the individual nor of his environment cover the total situation for the therapist. He must be aware of the interplay between the individual and his surroundings (the figure/ground), a position comparable to Sullivan's emphasis on interpersonal relations.

The authors go along with the shifting psychoanalytic emphasis from a search for repressed material to an investigation of the repressing forces in the individual (that is, the task of re-organizing the ego structure). Perls and associates point out that the neurotic feels his survival depends upon his continuing to repress, to censor, to defeat the therapist's efforts to penetrate his defenses. The repressing needs of the patient's ego can be reached not by therapeutic attack, the authors state, but by helping the patient and the therapist to understand the overlooked mechanisms whereby such repressing is accomplished. The "unfinished" (hence, neurotic) part of the patient is in the "obvious" functions of his being: the way he moves, talks, breathes, etc. The therapist must help him to understand the overlooked obvious things about himself in order to enable him to finish the Gestalt of his personality. The patient can regain the elastic figure/ground relation, which is the process of growth and maturing, and thus develop his "self" only by therapeutic guidance in re-examining the obvious about himself.

In their approach to therapy, Perls and his co-authors stress the need for a non-dogmatic, experimental situation. They feel that any implicit or explicit demands on the patient are not only likely to be futile, but may possibly be damaging. They present, instead, graded experiments which are designed to bring difficulties to the attention of the patient. What interferes with the effective accomplishment of the task becomes the focus of their work. They feel they thus bring out the patient's resistances and help him to work them through without directly challenging his defenses.

The types of experiments conducted by the authors are amply illustrated in their book. Without the step-by-step instructions for the exercises themselves and the reasoning which leads up to their use, description of them is either meaningless or misleading. It seemed wisest, therefore, not to try to present examples of these experimental procedures.

Unlike the Freudian approach of trying to recover something from the past or of rescuing it from behind character armor (Reich), Perls and his associates feel they lead their patients to make a creative adjustment to the given present situation. To complete the Gestalt in the present situation the patient must destroy and assimilate the unawareness as an obstacle. The therapeutic experiments allegedly bring out sharp delineation and precise verbal description of the disrupting block or void and open up ways to overcome it. The neurotic loses contact with reality and does not know how to regain it. He persists in a course that further removes him from actuality. The therapist helps him to learn (through the experiments) how he (the patient) is out of contact with reality, where and what the actuality now is, and how to keep in contact with it. Once the self of the patient can keep in contact and keep going, the therapy is terminated. A new and elastic figure/ground relation has thus been achieved.

C. HYPNOTHERAPY

Hypnosis has been both accepted and rejected many times by professional circles. One contemporary psychotherapist who has brought hypnotic techniques back to a status of respectability is Lewis R. Wolberg.

Wolberg believes that hypnosis by itself has no permanent psychotherapeutic effect, but that it functions well in conjunction with other therapeutic techniques. The chief values of hypnosis are its increase in the patient's suggestibility and its removal of repressions which (in the waking state) keep certain aspects of the personality from awareness. The former is quite helpful in the short-term, re-educative type of therapy, and the latter may be of assistance in depth-oriented, reconstructive therapy.

One type of therapeutic situation where the use of hypnosis may be advantageous is where a neurotic symptom is so destructive or incapacitating to the patient that it makes progress in psychotherapy difficult or impossible. The symptom can sometimes be at least temporarily removed by hypnosis at the same time that the patient is motivated to accept deeper therapy. Those kinds of symptoms most responsive to suggestive removal are hysterical symptoms (such as tics, paralysis, aphonia, amnesia, visual disorders, and other sensory disturbances) and habit disorders (insomnia, nail-biting, over-eating, and excessive smoking).

In re-educative therapy the goal is to lead the patient to an understanding of his distortions in interpersonal relationships and to help him toward a more harmonious integration with his environment. Hypnosis may be used to inculcate in the patient new adaptive goals and attitudes that are in line with his biosocial needs. Wolberg believes that there are some patients, such as many obsessive-compulsive personalities, who respond better to persuasion via hypnosis than to psychoanalysis. He believes that the substitution of persuasive philosophical precepts for destructive habit patterns is to be considered preferable to no treatment at all.

The use of hypnosis in reconstructive or psychoanalytic therapy (hypnoanalysis) is most helpful in reducing or removing resistance. Wolberg reports that the mere induction of a trance may be sufficient to bring repressed elements to awareness, but generally special techniques are required. Some of the techniques used are dream induction, automatic writing, dramatic acting out, mirror gazing, free association in trance, hypnotic drawing, the induction of experimental conflicts, and regression and revivification.

Wolberg states that transference feelings are often released during hypnosis and that their proper handling can be of great help in increasing the speed and effectiveness of the analysis. The integration of a memory regarding an earlier relationship with a parent (focused now on the therapist) into the patient's conscious life, and the understanding of feelings associated with the memory, can enable the patient to see what is happening in current life situations, according to the theory of Wolberg. In addition he feels that the recovery of traumatic memories may serve as a means of creating an incentive for change.

Hypnoanalysis also has its re-educational uses. An attempt is made to help the patient to gain insight into the dynamic unconscious sources of his difficulties. The chief technique involved here is for the therapist to demonstrate to him the meanings of his symptoms in terms of repressed conflict by inducing experimental conflicts in the course of the hypnotic trance.

Wolberg feels that hypnotherapy has definite limitations, some of which are as follows: not all patients can be hypnotized to the necessary depth; the material revealed may be fantasy and not true memory (and the two are not readily distinguished by the therapist); regression in hypnosis may seriously affect the transference situation; material encountered in the trance must be integrated in the more conscious layers of the psyche; and hypnosis is more useful in such conditions as hysteria and traumatic neuroses, than with character disorders.

D. EXPERIENTIAL THERAPY

Carl A. Whitaker, Thomas P. Malone, and their associates in the Atlanta Psychiatric Clinic have made a number of original contributions to psychotherapeutic theory and practice. They have specified that they are not interested in developing a new school of psychotherapy, but their ideas are sufficiently unified and distinct to be viewed as a "system."

Whitaker and Malone feel that psychotherapy in the broad sense includes any acceleration in the growth of a human being as a person. They limit their psychotherapeutic focus to growth in the sense of integration, and they feel that increased integration is expressed as both more maturity and as greater adequacy. That branch of psychotherapy which most concerns itself with the patient's deficits in maturity is the biologically based, the medical; and that division which concentrates on the deficit in adequacy is the interpersonal, social-scientific. The authors place their emphasis on matters of maturity because they feel this aspect of psychotherapy is currently in need of expansion. Their point of view may in many respects be considered as a return, with a fresh outlook, to the concerns of early psychoanalysis: that which has since been termed, "id psychology."

Although increased adequacy ordinarily develops through an educative social experience (these authors maintain), growth in maturity derives from emotional experiences. Alterations in the person's intrapersonal structures, the increasing ease in the exchange of energies within an individual, are the goal of experiential therapy. The patient who has had his dynamics rendered more flexible by emotional experiences and thus has energy freed from conflict to use in his interpersonal relations will probably need instruction in the more effective utilization of this energy, but Whitaker and Malone are not at this time primarily concerned with the adequacy aspect of therapy (which corresponds to what, in psychoanalytic circles, is called "ego psychology").

The essential dynamics of psychotherapy, according to Whitaker and associates, develop within a current experience. The psychotherapeutic experience modifies the pattern of inter-relationship of other current experiences and integrates the biological effects of previous experiences on the organization of current experience (hence the label "experiential therapy"). Such experience is essentially emotional (dealing with the id processes) rather than analytical, historical, genetic and logically causal (ego-level).

When such id-level therapy is functioning effectively, the therapist sees the patient (emotionally) as the child-self of the therapist. The needs of the therapist are intrapersonal ones which lead the therapist to achieve a better integration of his own self through this child-image of himself (the patient). Thus therapy, as these therapists conceive it, is really an externalized intrapersonal relationship: the therapist and a projection of himself. The experience is in this way isolated from reality for the patient and frees him temporarily from the roles demanded of him from society. He is able to act out fantasy roles never previously possible, which releases energy formerly bound in emotional conflict.

The therapist, meantime, is bringing to bear upon the patient the feelings and motivations from his own experience which he has perceived in a positive light and which he associates with the role of good parent. This enables the patient to deepen his symbolic involvement with the therapist. The therapist, seeing the patient as part of himself and the experience as a means of satisfying his own deeper integrative needs, has a feeling of growing significance and urgency to accelerate the growth of the patient.

As the therapist and the patient become increasingly emotionally involved in the therapeutic experience, a point is reached where each is responding maximally to the unconscious of the other. The level of communication is primitive (what Freud called the primary process) and consists essentially of mass body sensations. This stage of therapy is what Whitaker and Malone call a joint fantasy experience for the patient and the therapist and is, they believe, the point at which the main therapeutic benefits accrue to the patient. By fantasy they mean a pervasive experiencing of the unconscious in its totality (which is non-verbal and organic). The patient's acceptance of his own fantasies and unconscious experiences is facilitated because he has them in the presence of one who implicitly participates in them. This also, it is believed, leads to the development of a greater continuity between consciousness and unconsciousness and an increasing capacity for the realization of the patient's fundamental biological needs. The patient acquires from the therapist the realization that one can be fantastic while, at the same time, having a very adequate reality capacity.

Whitaker and Malone are reluctant to speak of specific techniques in psychotherapy because they feel that these should grow out of the uniquely personal way in which an individual therapist relates to his patients. They do, however, discuss methods they have found useful in facilitating the emotional, symbolic process of psychotherapy.

In the beginning phase of therapy, techniques should be primarily directed toward isolating the therapeutic experience from other experiences in order to hasten the production of symbolic, fantastic, and unconscious meanings. One useful way to achieve this isolation is for the therapist to delete as many realities as possible from the experience (refusal to discuss his real life, to answer the telephone during therapy, to talk over the patient's problems with his family or with the referring physician, etc.).

It is very important that the therapist indicate to the patient his awareness of the patient's maturities, his wellness, as well as his immaturities, his sickness. In this fashion, the patient's conception of his immaturities becomes less threatening.

The therapist should indicate to the patient that he will not permit his own (the therapist's) personal life to be exploited by the patient. It is important for the patient to see that the therapist is a person who has sufficient integrity and cognizance of his own separateness and realness to refuse to sacrifice himself in the fantasy relationship with the patient. Thus the patient's own confidence is increased about eventually emerging well from the fantasy relationship.

The patient also gains confidence for the plunge into fantasy by the therapist's presenting his own limitations and his immaturities. Again the patient is reassured that a healthy distinction between reality and fantasy is made by the therapist and can be achieved in the future by the patient.

Whitaker and Malone feel that most often, in the beginning phase of therapy, the therapist's responses should consist mainly in his implicit understanding of the symbolic meaning of what the patient has said or done. This implicit understanding can best be expressed in silence. Silence is particularly effective in discouraging mere intellectual verbiage which has no real emotional significance for the patient. A non-verbal response by the therapist to the patient serves the purpose of helping the patient to hear his own superficial verbalization most clearly and precipitates the patient into a deeper level of transference. It also aids the therapist in the development of his own fantasy participation in the relationship.

Both aggression in various forms and physical contact can be judiciously used by the therapist, according to the authors. They agree, however, that these techniques are most likely to be abused and should not be undertaken by the inexperienced therapist.

Much emphasis is placed by the authors on the joint fantasy experience as an aid to effective deep level communication between the patient and the therapist. They have utilized such material objects as clay and rubber knives and such techniques as sleeping and dreaming in the therapeutic sessions as means of facilitating fantasy participation. (The therapist will have a dream in the course of therapy which he then, on awakening, recounts to the patient. The dream presumably helps "clear things up" for therapist and patient.)

Perhaps it is fair to summarize the whole philosophy and procedure of experiential therapy with the statement that the therapist says, in depth effect, to the patient: "We are both troubled people; let us see if by entering the world of fantasy together we can help one another to do a better job of fulfilling our true selves and thus to emerge again in the external world more capable of handling the problems of reality."

E. CONDITIONED REFLEX THERAPY

A radical departure from the usual theories and practices of psychotherapy is the conditioned reflex therapy of Andrew Salter. As the term suggests, this therapy is the application of the Pavlovian conditioning process to clinical procedures. Holding that man's behavior is inseparably rooted in his animal nature, Salter feels that neurotic behavior can be rendered healthy by direct re-conditioning (strong positive suggestion). Salter not only finds more refined and intellectualized procedures futile and irrelevant, but likely further to entrench the person's emotional illness.

The basis of life, according to Salter, is excitation. The cause of emotional illness is inhibition. Hence, the role of the therapist is to help persons to overcome their inhibitions and to express their real feelings. The emotionally ill person has, in one way or another, experienced inhibiting conditioning and needs to be encouraged to develop his excitatory reflexes. Although Salter admits that living in society calls for some inhibition, he feels that the inhibiting conditioning aspects of our culture go far beyond the point needed and thus produce emotional illness. The many different forms of such illness, he contends, boil down to the same fundamental deprivation of excitation.

In his therapy, Salter instructs his clients to stop thinking and to start acting on the basis of their feelings. The healthy person, he believes, is one who acts on spontaneous, outgoing feeling: the healthy act without thinking, and the emotionally ill think without acting.

Salter has developed six basic techniques for reconditioning the faulty, inhibitory patterns of earlier life in the direction of excitation. The first of these disciplines, as he refers to them, is feeling-talk. Since man is a word-using animal, his basic means of excitation is through speech. By saying what he feels when he feels it (even at the risk of social disapproval), the patient will recondition himself away from inhibition and toward excitation.

Salter's second therapeutic discipline for his inhibited client is what he calls facial talk. He should, in other words, frankly show his emotions on his face—positive and negative alike.

The third technique in which Salter instructs his clients is that of contradiction and attack. The client is told not to act as if he agrees when he disagrees. Even without supporting evidence, the client should speak up with his feelings of disagreement and thus externalize his feelings.

Salter also tells his clients to use the word "I" deliberately as much as possible. This helps, he contends, in getting out excitatory feelings.

When praised (Salter suggests in his fifth precept), the client should express agreement. If someone says, for example: "That was a good speech you made at the Elk dinner last Friday," the client should reply along the following lines: "Yes, I think I was in top form that night. It seems to me it made a fine follow-up on your excellent speech of a year ago." Salter suggests the desirability of thus working in a returned compliment for the other person as well as reflecting favorably his praise of the client.

Salter's sixth rule of conduct is improvisation. His clients are instructed not to plan, but to live for the here and now. Planning leads to inhibition, he contends, so his already inhibited clients need rather to improvise actions from moment to moment and day to day than to encourage further inhibitory reflexes by stopping to think ahead.

For critics who suggest that excitation can be carried too far, Salter has the answer of "yes, but not by these inhibited clients." These overly inhibited people, he believes, need to learn to act as if they were constantly half-drunk. Then, if after they have become reconditioned to be excitatory instead of inhibitory personalities, they later need some toning down, that, Salter feels, is easily accomplished.

Salter holds, then, that the solution to all the problems brought to the therapist comes from helping the client to disinhibit (unbrake) his conditioned inhibitory emotional reflexes and thus to develop excitatory emotional reflexes. The client is thus re-educated to return to the healthy spontaneity of which his negative life experiences had deprived him. Such reconditioning of the individual is even deeper than other types of therapy, Salter holds, because it is more thoroughgoing. Maladjustment is malconditioning, as he sees it, and psychotherapy is effective reconditioning.

It is interesting that Salter has apparently developed no following among even behavioristically oriented psychologists. His methods are viewed as overly simplified and his claims of cures extravagant. Salter seems to feel that his critics are blinded to the truth of his theories and practices by the conditioning they have received from psychoanalysts and others who have led them to believe a lot of complicated nonsense about the human animal.

F. PSYCHOTHERAPY BY RECIPROCAL INHIBITION

A more recent, careful, and sophisticated application of the theories of conditioned response learning to the therapeutic setting is what

Joseph Wolpe, the originator, calls *psychotherapy by reciprocal inhibition*. Wolpe took his first psychotherapeutic cue from observations of experiments with animals. He noticed particularly that the neurotic behavior of an animal tends to disappear when the pleasurable experience of feeding occurs in the presence of anxiety-evoking stimuli. He inferred from these and other experimental findings that in general it is possible to overcome a habit by forming a new and antagonistic habit in the same stimulus situation.

Conducting human clinical investigations patterned along the same general lines as the animal experiments, Wolpe emerged with the following principle: if a response opposed to anxiety can be made to take place in the presence of anxiety-evoking stimuli so that a complete or partial suppression of the anxiety responses is effected, the bond between these stimuli and the anxiety responses will be weakened.

Wolpe did not try feeding responses for overcoming human neuroses; he found other responses more convenient: mainly, assertive responses, relaxation responses, and sexual responses. He has also successfully employed respiratory responses, conditioned motor responses, "anxiety relief" (electric shock cessation) responses, and conditioned avoidance responses. He has caused these responses to be called forth, inside and outside the consulting room, under conditions arranged so that the neurotic anxiety will be maximally inhibited by the antagonistic response selected.

For example, with the use of relaxation as the antagonistic response method to be employed, Wolpe first gives the patient preliminary training in relaxation. He also works out a list of stimuli to which the patient reacts with unadaptive anxiety. The stimuli are ranked according to the amount of disturbance they cause. The patient is then hypnotized, made to relax as deeply as possible, and told to imagine the weakest item in the list—what Wolpe calls the "smallest dose of phobic stimulation." In case the relaxation is not impaired by this dosage, a slightly greater one is presented at the next session. After a number of sessions of gradually increased dosage of phobic stimulation, the patient reaches the point, according to Wolpe, where the phobic stimulus can be presented at maximum intensity without impairing the calm and relaxed state. Then, in situations outside the therapeutic setting, the patient will stop reacting with his previous anxiety to the strongest of the once phobic stimuli. Therapy by reciprocal inhibition has thus taken place.

Wolpe offers statistics to support his assertion that his method has an almost 90 per cent efficiency in helping patients as compared with the 50 to 60 per cent credited to psychoanalytic and other methods. He even contends that much of the lesser success of other techniques derives from the *unknowing* application of reciprocal inhibition therapy. In the private interview (under any type of therapeutic procedure), Wolpe points out, the patient often has positive emotional responses as he confidentially reveals and talks about his difficulties to a person he believes to be knowledgeable, skillful, and desirous of helping him. If these emotional responses which tend to be antagonistic to anxiety are of sufficient strength, they will reciprocally inhibit the anxiety responses that are evoked by some of the subject matter of the interview. Therapeutic effects will thus occur. If, however, the emotional response is small (little transference, in analytic terms), positive results will probably not develop. Or, if too much anxiety is aroused by the interview, Wolpe points out, the patient may get worse.

Wolpe also believes that spontaneous cures of neurosis (where patients get over their neurotic symptoms without any form of treatment) are often the result of fortuitous reciprocal inhibition. He believes his system, in other words, more deliberately and efficiently applies the curative procedures that unsystematically take place in other forms of psychotherapy and in life outside the clinical setting. He invites the step-by-step testing of psychotherapy by reciprocal inhibition by other clinicians and says that a certain amount of such experimentation is already in process.

Summary

Six systems of psychotherapy were considered in this chapter: psychobiologic therapy, Gestalt therapy, hypnotherapy, experiential therapy, conditioned reflex therapy, and psychotherapy by reciprocal inhibition. Of the six, three (psychobiologic, Gestalt, and experiential) may be viewed as somewhat eclectic and integrative of a number of points of view, as well as containing original emphases. Hypnotherapy may be looked upon as largely adjunctive to other therapeutic techniques. Conditioned reflex therapy and psychotherapy by reciprocal inhibition are major departures from the general trend of psychotherapy.

In Meyer's psychobiologic therapy, much stress is placed on the importance of obtaining a clear and full understanding of the patient's own views of his problem, obtained by careful history taking. The therapist emphasizes for both himself and the patient that the clinical activity is a joint search for a desirable resolution of the patient's problems. In this search, the psychobiologist tries to remain flexible and eclectic regarding techniques. Much of his attention is directed toward helping the patient to overcome destructive habits and concomitant emotional attitudes (especially those reflecting self-hate and self-disrespect) which have irrationally imprisoned him from childhood.

Perls, Hefferline, and Goodman have tried to use the concepts of Gestalt psychology to work out a new integrative conception of human behavior and of the therapeutic treatment of this behavior. In the course of his contact with our culture, the Gestaltists contend, the average person gets his wholeness of thinking, feeling, and acting fragmented. Gestalt therapy is directed toward restoring this wholeness. While the authors draw on psychoanalytic and other concepts to further their theory and practice, much of their psychotherapy consists of graded experiments which are designed to bring difficulties progressively to the attention of the patient and to help him work out more realistic Gestalts of himself and his environment.

Wolberg uses hypnosis in the course of both re-educative and reconstructive (psychoanalytic) therapy. In the former, hypnosis is used to inculcate in the patient new and adaptive goals and attitudes that are in line with his biosocial needs. In hypnoanalysis the technique is most helpful in reducing or removing resistance. In the course of treating resistance he uses dream induction, free association in the trance, induction of experimental conflicts, regression, and a number of other hypnotic methods. He also feels that hypnoanalysis can be employed to assist the patient in gaining insight into the dynamic unconscious sources of his difficulties. He recognizes definite limitations, however, in hypnotic techniques and does not view them as replacements of other therapeutic methods.

While specifically disclaiming their desire to develop a new system, Whitaker and Malone have made a number of contributions to theory and technique under the heading of "experiential therapy." Their stress is placed on the emotional experiences of therapist and patient in the treatment situation. In this id-level therapy, the authors point out, the experience is isolated from reality, and the patient is encouraged to act out deep fantasy roles never previously possible. The therapist, meantime, brings to bear on the patient the feelings and motivations from his own experience which he has perceived in a positive light and which he associates with the role of good parent (the patient is felt to be a kind of projection of the therapist's own child self). Whitaker and Malone use a number of unusual techniques in their therapeutic procedures, which are a kind of joint venture of the therapist and patient into the primitive fantasy world of the unconscious.

The conditioned reflex therapy of Salter is based on an animalistic conception of man. The role of the therapist is to help persons to overcome their inhibitions (the source of their sickness, according to Salter) and to express their real feelings in an excitatory fashion. Such reconditioning of the individual is even deeper than other types of therapy, Salter holds, because it is more thorough-going. Maladjustment is malconditioning, as he sees it, and psychotherapy is effective reconditioning.

Wolpe's psychotherapy by reciprocal inhibition is similarly based on observations of animal learning by conditioned response, but consists of more careful and sophisticated applications of principles thus derived to the human clinical setting. Wolpe's major therapeutic principle is that the bond between certain stimuli and anxiety responses can be weakened by the simultaneous evoking of responses antagonistic to anxiety. He not only offers considerable support for his own procedures of reciprocal inhibition in therapy, but also contends that much of the success of other psychotherapies and of spontaneous cures derives from the fortuitous occurrence of similar conditioning.

Selected Readings

Muncie, Wendell, *Psychobiology and Psychiatry*. St. Louis: Mosby, 1939.

Perls, Frederick, Ralph Hefferline, and Paul Goodman. *Gestalt Therapy*. New York: Julian Press, 1951.

Salter, Andrew, *Conditioned Reflex Therapy*. New York: Creative Age Press, 1949.

Whitaker, C. A., and T. P. Malone, *The Roots of Psychotherapy*. New York: McGraw, 1953.

Winters, E. C. (Ed), *The Collected Papers of Adolf Meyer* (3 vols). Baltimore: Johns Hopkins, 1950-52.

Wolberg, Lewis R., *Medical Hypnosis* (2 vols). New York: Grune, 1948.

Wolpe, Joseph, *Psychotherapy by Reciprocal Inhibition*. Stanford, Calif.: Stanford, 1958.

CHAPTER **8**

A Variety of Systems: II

Five more systems of psychotherapy will be treated in this chapter. These are directive psychotherapy, general semantics, learning theory therapy, assertion-structured therapy, and rational therapy. All of these therapies constitute marked departures from the therapeutic mode of psychoanalysis.

A. DIRECTIVE PSYCHOTHERAPY

The first of these systems which we shall consider is not so much a reaction against psychoanalysis, however, as an antidote to what its originator, Frederick Thorne, considers the unhealthy, cultish popularity of Rogersian nondirective (client-centered) therapy. Thorne, both a clinical psychologist and a psychiatrist, views his approach as eclectic, not a new system in itself. His use of the term "directive" does not mean that he feels there are not times when permissive, nondirective responses are appropriate. But the term emphasizes Thorne's conviction that constant nondirectiveness and passivity are inappropriate and that *direction* of the therapeutic process belongs in the hands of the skilled therapist and not the sick patient.

Thorne points out that, in general, the need for direction is inversely correlated with the person's ability for effective self-regulation. The sicker the personality, the greater the need for direction from the therapist. Because, in the hands of some unskilled therapists, directive procedures have sometimes been misused, nondirectivists have made the mistaken judgment, according to Thorne, of believing that direction in any form is undesirable.

Thorne feels that directive psychotherapy requires the therapist to be trained and able to use every known method, including some recently neglected ones like hypnosis, suggestion, reconditioning, and direct reassurance. He believes in genuine eclecticism which makes possible the use of all technical resources, either directive or nondirective, that are available at the time and place and seem appropriate to the particular patient's needs.

The directive psychotherapist, unlike the nondirective, develops a specific plan of action. He makes adequate diagnostic studies, including complete case histories, clinical examinations, psychometric and projective studies, and laboratory procedures (such as electroencephalography). The directivist also prepares a descriptive formulation of the psychodynamics of each case: etiology, clinical status, personality resources, and prognosis. His plan makes use of the principles of experimental science wherever applicable at all levels of case handling.

Thorne's directive psychotherapy is based on several premises, which may be summarized as follows: (1) When society, family, the school, and the patient himself have failed to condition healthy behavior the therapist steps in as a kind of master educator. (2) The creation of suitable conditions for the patient to learn a new style of life is the first task of the therapist. This involves the establishment of rapport, analysis of past traumatic conditions, release of emotional blocks, and encouragement of the patient in his own problem-solving processes. (3) Science provides the most valid and reliable authority for interference directively in the life of the patient (as contrasted with earlier arbitrary and unverifiable authority of the church, the family, the government, etc.). Broad scientific training provides the highest standards of competence for the therapist, and help for the patient most favorably arises from this source rather than from emotional, intuitive impressions of either therapist or patient.

Thorne objects to the application of the term "client-centered" to therapy which is strictly nondirectively oriented. He states that intelligently conceived directive therapy is more likely to be centered directly upon the client's real needs than therapy which uses the client's own (sick) feelings as the chief guide. The directively oriented therapy must be client-centered, according to Thorne, with the therapist interjecting only as may be needed to keep the client headed in constructive directions.

B. GENERAL SEMANTICS

Problems in communication are observable in most, if not all, forms of emotional disturbance. It is understandable, then, that attempts would be made to apply the findings of semantics to the theories and techniques of psychotherapy. Semantics is the scientific study of the relations between signs (symbols) and what they mean, and of behavior in its psychological and sociological aspects as it is influenced by signs.

Alfred Korzybski and Wendell Johnson are two semanticists who have made serious efforts (separately) to apply their studies to psychotherapy. Korzybski has postulated that neurotic behavior stems from a lack of clear understanding in the use of words and their meanings. Vagueness in phrasing and defects in conceptualization, among other things, are characteristic of the mentally ill person. So long as there is lack of clarity in the use of symbols, the individual is unable to define or think critically about his values and life goals. Therapy consists primarily in teaching the patient the correct word-habits to replace the faulty orientations in language he previously acquired. He then becomes increasingly able to substitute reality-oriented ends and means for self-defeating patterns.

Wendell Johnson points out that the emotionally disturbed person talks and thinks himself into conflicts. The patient's maladjustments are often the product of unrealistic ideals in life which bring about frustration. Consistent frustration leads to demoralization. Part of the difficulty arises from the patient's inability to conceptualize clearly what he wants from life, and he is, therefore, bound to be disappointed with whatever he achieves. The patient's problems are persistent and cumulative, too, because he cannot identify them properly as a result of his poor organization and clarity of language. The use of semantics in therapy, according to Johnson, is to retrain the patient in the meaning of words about himself and his environment.

As the patient becomes capable of conceiving and formulating his problems more clearly, he gains confidence in his ability to communicate with others and, hence, to handle his interpersonal relations with increasing effectiveness.

While the focus of general semantics may be different from other systems of psychotherapy, it obviously must draw upon techniques developed by other systems. Strict concentration on words and their meaning would seem to be unlikely to achieve removal of all symptoms in highly disturbed patients. The semanticist-therapist strives to improve the communication of his patient with himself, with the therapist, and with others. Attention is also necessarily given to rapport, transference, resistance, and other matters common to other therapeutic orientations. The semantic emphasis has, however, brought to the attention of therapists of other systems the need for greater study and work with communication problems of their patients.

C. LEARNING THEORY THERAPY

A number of psychologists have attempted to view psychotherapy in terms of learning theory. We shall not try to list all of the variations in their views or to attach names of psychologists to variations. Instead, we present a broad overview of learning theory therapy. Names of psychologists who have considerably contributed to this type of therapy follow: John Dollard, Neal Miller, O. H. Mowrer, George Kelly, Julian Rotter, and E. J. Shoben, Jr.

Learning is the summarizing name for all the processes by means of which an individual is changed so that at a later time his actions or reactions are not what they would have been without the previous activity. These modifications in the individual may be favorable or unfavorable. Much of what we have variously labeled emotional disturbance, mental illness, neurosis, psychosis, apparently derives from unfavorable learning experiences. All of the things we have considered under the general category of psychotherapy represent attempts (though not always successful) at promoting favorable learning experiences. Learning theory therapists have tried in their various ways, therefore, to apply psychological knowledge of the nature of both favorable and unfavorable learning to the problems of psychotherapy and its treatment of emotional disturbances.

Learning theory shows us in some detail why a maladjusted person does not automatically learn adjustive behavior. The Freudian concept of the pleasure principle is translated into the learning concept of reinforcement. Much of the maladjusted person's behavior may be understood as that of avoiding that which, as a result of learning experience in his past carries with it (for him) painful reactions. He repeats the avoidant behavior patterns which keep him out of the situations or experiences where he could learn more adjustive behavior. Psychotherapy, therefore, becomes primarily a process of leading the individual into new situations and experiences and controlling as much as possible the nature of those new experiences to increase the probability of gratification. Once the patient experiences gratification from the new learning, the new and more adjustive behavior patterns will be reinforced in the same fashion that the old and less adjustive behavior patterns were.

One of the most effective types of reinforcement is anxiety reduction. Since the patient who decides to undergo psychotherapy is generally so filled with anxiety that he has come to realize (often with desperation) that he can no longer manage without help, he is an especially adept subject for unlearning old behavior patterns. This is true because the reinforcing effect of the old patterns has already been reduced by their breakdown in the life situations which led him to undertake psychotherapy. He is also more susceptible to learning new patterns, which, if the therapist is skillful, can be rendered more quickly and efficiently sources of gratification than without such therapeutic guidance.

The psychoanalytic concept of transference can also be largely understood in terms of the learning theory concept of generalization. The individual develops habitual patterns of response by the process of generalization; that is, responses learned in one particular situation are brought out in what are (often childishly and superficially) identified as similar situations. If the child has many frustrating experiences with what he comes to perceive as an unloving, prudish, frustrating, castrating (in the symbolic sense) mother, he is apt (unless he has some strongly corrective experience with another type of woman concurrently) to develop the generalized concept that all women, not just his mother, possess these disturbing characteristics). Many of his maladaptive behavior patterns can then be understood in terms of this generalized learning, and much of the task of the psychotherapist would be that of directing the patient into social experiences that would be conducive to "unlearning" this concept of women and developing a new and more adjustive concept.

In learning theory terms, much of psychotherapy consists in unlearning or "counterconditioning" the anxieties that motivate compulsive, neurotic behavior (that is, self-perpetuating, self-defeating behavior patterns). Maladaptive behavior patterns are considered largely those which temporarily reduce anxiety, but do nothing about changing the conditions that have produced anxiety. The main reason such self-defeating patterns tend to be self-perpetuating is that they offer the means of immediate reduction of anxiety. The disturbed person, confused by his anxiety, is not able to achieve the perspective necessary to see beyond his emotionally confused state. He keeps doing the things that bring a short-run reduction of his anxiety even though he is simultaneously reaping a long-run increase in anxiety. The learning theory therapists have labeled this principle the "gradient of reinforcement," which hypothesizes that the consequences of actions that lie closest in time to their performance will have the greatest effect. Thus, the immediate relief of acutely painful anxiety leads the emotionally disturbed person to do over and over again what (in the long run) is a self-defeating procedure. The chief task of the learning theory therapist is to break up such self-perpetuating, self-defeating procedures and help the individual to find new patterns which will lead him to full self-realization. In one variant application of learning theory, role playing is employed as the chief tool for accomplishing this therapeutic task. By learning a new social role, the patient may develop a new outlook on his problems and thus deal with them more effectively.

Learning theorists are usually quite active and directive in their therapy. Intervention of direct interpretation is usually considered the most effective way of reducing reinforcement of the older, undesirable patterns and of increasing reinforcement of the newer, more adjustive patterns. Emphasis is also placed on the corrective and reinforcing value of experiences between therapeutic sessions, and much of the time in the actual sessions is directed toward improving the expectancy of favorable reinforcement of the newer patterns in the everyday life experiences of the patient.

Probably more than any other group of therapists, learning theory therapists have rested their contentions on inferences about human behavior that derive from scientific studies. As a group, therefore, they tend to be more cautious, less inclined toward broad claims and sweeping generalizations. They point consistently to the need for further study, to the incompleteness of learning hypotheses, to the tentative applications of existing hypotheses to human behavior in general and to psychotherapy in particular. Such therapists do hold, however, that the behavior of greatest interest to the therapist is learned: negatively, in the form of disturbances presented for treatment; positively, in the form of therapeutic procedures to be undertaken. Since such behavior is learned, these psychologists point out, it must be learned in accordance with principles of learning, known or unknown, and not by any special, mystical process. Further collaboration between the experimental learning psychologist and the psychotherapist would, therefore, seem desirable for all parties concerned.

D. ASSERTION-STRUCTURED THERAPY

E. Lakin Phillips is a psychologist who has attempted to bring the theory and practice of psychotherapy more in line with the findings of contemporary academic and experimental psychology. He has deliberately developed a non-depth theory, which he calls "the interference theory," and the therapy based on this view of human behavior he names "assertion-structured therapy."

Phillips contends that behavioral possibilities are selected by the perceiving-acting person to meet the situations that confront him rather than being the function of his "depths," his unconscious mind. The behavior patterns of any person are to be understood in terms of the choices he makes; he lives by what Phillips calls his *assertions* about the situations in which he finds himself. The individual's assertions (the hypotheses by which he lives; the assumptions on which he operates) have varying probabilities of confirmation or disconfirmation. Hence, life is a constant actuarial process; the individual is betting on his assertions and winning (confirmation) or losing (disconfirmation). The neurotic is essentially a person who is constantly betting on a set of assertions that have a high probability of disconfirmation. The neurotic's behavior, in fact, becomes what Phillips calls redundant—that is, he tends to repeat certain patterns in a circular, self-defeating way. The stronger the assertion, the greater the redundancy; the greater the redundancy, the more inflexible is the organism.

When a patient comes to a therapist, he has been experiencing failure in life. He has, in Phillips' terms, been betting on assertions with poor odds in favor of being confirmed in reality. The therapist's main job, then, is to interfere with what the person is doing, with the kind or degree of his assertions, and to teach the patient to bet less or to bet on different assertions—namely, ones that have greater probability of being confirmed.

This type of therapy, Phillips states, can be conducted on a relatively simple, practical, economical, and efficient basis. When the goal is that of helping the patient to shift his behavior patterns from assertions that hold small probability of confirmation to those that hold high probability, no elaborate hypotheses or complicated terms or long periods of time are necessary.

Psychopathology is understood in Phillips' thinking largely in terms of tension which results from conflict. When the person's assertions meet with frequent disconfirmation, the person and his environment are in conflict. The persistence of such conflict brings both physiological and psychological symptoms and syndromes, the presence of which in an individual leads the therapist to classify him as neurotic, psychotic, emotionally disturbed, mentally ill, etc. If the conflict is not soon resolved, and the tension thus continues to grow, the redundancy of behavior referred to earlier results, for the tension narrows the individual's problem-solving potential. The task of psychotherapy is to reduce the redundant condition of disconfirmation and the resulting tension, so that the individual can engage in effective problem-solving and thus be more firmly oriented in reality. And this, as stated above, is chiefly accomplished by the therapeutic process of interference with ongoing behavior and by teaching substitute patterns that hold greater probability of environmental confirmation. Focus on this procedure is the therapist's main job.

E. RATIONAL PSYCHOTHERAPY

Another very recent systematic psychotherapeutic development has evolved from the clinical practice of a New York psychologist and former psychoanalyst, Albert Ellis. Ellis calls his system "rational psychotherapy." Although influenced by his earlier analytic orientation (which was, however, broadly eclectic and critical of the psychoanalytic departures from science), Ellis' theoretical formulations and techniques may be considered to a great extent a repudiation of not only classical psychoanalysis, but of even the more liberalized approaches of the dynamic culturalists. Probably the closest approach Ellis makes to any system associated with psychoanalysis is to the individual psychology of Adler, but the similarities were reached by quite dissimilar routes.

Rational psychotherapy starts with the hypothesis that human emotion is most importantly caused and controlled by thinking. Much of what is labeled emotion, Ellis contends, is a biased, prejudiced, or strongly evaluative type of thought, and thought usually takes place in terms of language. The individual who feels positive emotions, therefore, such as love or elation, is usually saying to himself, consciously or unconsciously, some sentence to the effect that "this is good." In negative emotions, such as anger or depression, the feeling is caused by some form or variation of the sentence "this is terrible." If an adult did not employ, on some conscious or unconscious level, such sentences, Ellis holds, much of his emoting simply would not exist.

If human emotions largely result from thinking, as Ellis suggests, then one may appreciably control one's feelings by controlling one's thoughts. That is, a person may change the nature of his feelings from negative to positive (or neutral) by changing the internalized sentences, or self-talk, with which he largely created the feelings in the first place. This is what the rational therapist teaches his clients to do: to understand exactly how they create their own emotional reactions by telling themselves certain things, and how they can create different emotional reactions by telling themselves other things.

Ellis believes that emotional disturbance essentially arises when individuals mentally reiterate negative, unrealistic, illogical, self-defeating thoughts. He further believes that, for the most part, disturbed individuals are not aware that they are talking to themselves illogically, or of what the irrational links in their internalized sentences are, or of how they can learn to tell themselves saner and more realistic thoughts or sentences. That is why much of the rational therapist's work is helping the client to find out what he is now saying in the way of internalized sentences, to question the rationality of what he discovers he is saying, and to substitute more rational, more realistic, and more positive self-talk.

Athough Ellis grants that some of man's illogical ideas may be rooted in his biological limitations, most of them derive from his upbringing. A person in our society gets most of his irrational self-sentences from his parents, his teachers, his peer group, and his contact with the general culture, especially through mass media. It is virtually impossible, Ellis points out, to grow up in our society today without an over-abundance of illogical ideas and philosophies which inescapably lead to a certain amount of self-defeating patterns or neurosis.

There are many illogical internalized statements that Ellis feels are very commonplace in our culture. He states that usually several of these almost universal, self-defeating sentences (along with some individualized ones) can be found in any patient who reports for therapy. We present here only a few of what Ellis maintains to be commonly held irrational beliefs. The "illogical" idea which leads to human self-defeat and neurosis is presented first (a) and the more reasonable substitute that the rational therapist attempts to inculcate is given second (b).

1. (a) It is a dire necessity for an adult to be approved or loved by almost everyone for almost everything he does. It is most important what others think of one. It is better to depend on others than on oneself, for a self-sufficient person is a selfish person.

(b) It is pleasant, but not necessary, for an adult to be approved or loved by others. It is better to win one's own respect than others' approval. It is more desirable to stand on one's own feet than to depend mainly on others.

2. (a) It is terrible, horrible, and catastrophic when things are

not the way one would like them to be; they *should* be better than they are. Others should make things easier for one, help with life's difficulties. One should not have to put off present pleasures for future gains.

(b) It is too bad when things are not the way one would like them to be, and one should try to change conditions for the better; but when this is impossible, one had better become resigned to the way things are and stop pointless complaining. It is nice when others help one with life's difficulties; but if they don't, that is too bad and one can confront these difficulties oneself. If one does not often put off present pleasures for future gain, one sabotages one's own well-being.

3. (a) It is easier to avoid than to face life difficulties and self-responsibilities. Inertia and inaction are necessary and/or pleasant. One should rebel against doing things, however necessary, if it is unpleasant to do them.

(b) The so-called easier way is usually the much harder way in the long run, and the only way to solve difficult problems is to face them squarely. Inertia and inaction are generally unnecessary and relatively unpleasant: humans tend to be happiest when they are actively and vitally absorbed in creative pursuits. One should do necessary things, however unpleasant they may be, without complaining and rebelling.

Ellis contends that rational therapy, though usually a briefer procedure than psychoanalysis, is in some respects more depth-centered and intensive because it seeks to reveal and assail the basic ideas or philosophies or values which underlie neurosis. Although in that sense depth-oriented, the rational therapist focuses his attention on what he believes are the current, not the past, causes of the emotional disturbance. He shows the client that his problems, especially his negative feelings (such as anger, depression, anxiety, and guilt), arise not from past events or external situations but from his present irrational attitudes toward or illogical fears about these events and situations. Thus a client is shown that it is not his Oedipal attachment which made and keeps him neurotic, but his self-perpetuated illogical ideas underlying this attachment: his groundless beliefs that he is wicked for lusting after his mother, that he cannot survive without his mother's and father's love, that he will be castrated by his father, that it is horrible to have others think him incestuous, etc.

The rational therapist emphasizes *self-interest* in his treatment procedures. One should love one's neighbor, or at least take care not to harm him, not out of any moral authoritarianism, but out of self-interest: namely, only by so doing is one likely to help build the kind of society in which one would best live *oneself*. The rational therapist believes, in other words, that self-interest demands social interest; and that the rational individual who strives for his own happiness will, for that very reason, also be interested in others. Ellis also believes (along with Fromm and others) that the human animal normally and naturally is helpful and loving to other humans, provided that it is not enmeshed in illogical thinking that leads it to self-destructive, self-hating behavior.

Ellis frequently employs the usual expressive-emotive, supportive, relationship, and insight-interpretative techniques, especially early in the therapy, but he considers these methods merely preparatory to his main task. While most therapists directly or indirectly show the client that he is behaving illogically, the rational therapist makes a forthright, unequivocal *attack* on the client's general and specific irrational ideas and tries to *induce* him to adopt more rational ones in their place.

There are two main ways, according to Ellis, that the rational therapist makes a concerted attack on the disturbed individual's irrational positions: (a) the therapist serves as a frank counter-propagandist who directly contradicts and denies the self-defeating propaganda and superstitions which the client originally learned and keeps perpetuating. (b) The therapist encourages, persuades, cajoles, and at times commands the client to engage in some kind of activity which itself will act as a forceful counter-propagandistic agency against the nonsense he believes. Both of these therapeutic acts are consciously performed with the goal of finally getting the client to internalize a rational philosophy of living just as he originally internalized the irrational ideas and attitudes of his parents, siblings, peer group, and general culture.

Rational psychotherapy, Ellis says, is like most other systems in working best with individuals who are not too psychotic, who are fairly intelligent, and who are reasonably young when they come for treatment. The traits most positively related to successful outcome, Ellis has tentatively stated, are a willingness to work, intellectual curiosity, and a willingness to accept direction from the therapist at the beginning. Among those who benefit least from rational therapy, at this point in its development, are clients who will not accept hard work and discipline, who refuse to try to think for themselves, and who dogmatically insist on adhering to some absolutist creed, such as orthodox Freudianism.

Summary

Directive psychotherapy, general semantics, learning theory therapy, assertion-structured therapy, and rational psychotherapy were the five systems treated in Chapter 8. All five constitute marked departures from the psychoanalytic mode.

Thorne's directive therapy is mainly a reaction against what he considers the extremist, nondirective tendencies of client-centered therapy. He emphasizes that the direction of the therapeutic process belongs in the hands of the skilled therapist and not the sick patient. In helping the patient to work out a new style of life, a more effective pattern of living, Thorne believes in drawing upon any technique or resource legitimately available to the therapist. This includes the utilization of various diagnostic tools and a therapeutic plan of action based as nearly as possible on scientific observations of human behavior in general and the patient's behavior in particular.

General semantics consists of the attempt to apply "knowledge of symbols and their meaning and influence on human behavior" to the therapeutic situation. Korzybski has postulated that neurotic behavior stems from a lack of clear understanding in the use of words and their meanings, and his therapy consists primarily in teaching the patient the correct word-habits to replace the faulty orientations in language he previously acquired. In like manner, Wendell Johnson has contended that the emotionally disturbed person talks and thinks himself into conflicts and that therapy is chiefly a matter of retraining the patient in the meaning of the words he applies to himself and his environment. While relatively few therapists consider themselves primarily semanticists, the work of Korzybski, Johnson, and other semanticists has influenced other therapists in undertaking greater study and work with communication problems.

Learning theory psychologists have suggested that much of psychotherapy consists in "unlearning" or "counter-conditioning" the anxieties that motivate the self-defeating, self-perpetuating behavior patterns in neurotics. The major work of the therapist, as thus conceived, is to break up the attitudes that are acting as reinforcements of these self-defeating patterns. Interjection of direct interpretation is usually considered the most effective way of reducing reinforcement of the older, undesirable patterns and of increasing reinforcement of the newer, more adjustive patterns. Emphasis is also placed on the corrective and reinforcing value of experiences between therapeutic sessions.

The main contention of Phillips' assertion-structured therapy is that the behavior patterns of any person are to be understood in terms of the choices he makes. He lives by what Phillips calls his *assertions* about the situations in which he finds himself. When his assertions meet with frequent disconfirmation in his interpersonal relations, he develops the redundant, self-defeating behavior of the neurotic. Therapy consists largely in interfering with these self-defeating patterns of the individual and helping to develop behavior based on assertions that have much greater probability of being confirmed in his day-by-day interactions.

It is Ellis' main thesis, in what he calls rational psychotherapy, that emotion in the adult human being is most importantly caused and controlled by thinking. The disturbed individual has adopted a lot of irrational and illogical ideas that cause him to behave in a neurotic or psychotic fashion. The job of the therapist is to help the disturbed individual to become aware of the verbalizations he delivers to himself in becoming distressed, point out the stupidity of such self-sayings, and help the person to adopt more rational points of view. When this is achieved, according to Ellis, the individual will cease to be emotionally disturbed.

Selected Readings

Dollard, John, and Neal E. Miller, *Personality and Psychotherapy*. New York: McGraw, 1950.

Ellis, Albert, *How to Live with a Neurotic*. New York: Crown, 1957.

———, "Outcome of Employing Three Techniques of Psychotherapy," *Journal of Clinical Psychology*, 1957, 23, 344-350.

Johnson, Wendell, *People in Quandaries*. New York: Harper, 1946.

Kelly, George, *The Psychology of Personal Constructs* (2 vols). New York: Norton, 1955.

Korzybski, Alfred, *Science and Sanity*. Lancaster, Pa.: Science Press, 1941.

Mowrer, O. H., *Learning Theory and Personality Dynamics*. New York: Ronald, 1950.

Phillips, E. Lakin, *Psychotherapy: A Modern Theory and Practice*. Englewood Cliffs, N. J.: Prentice-Hall, 1956.

Rotter, Julian B., *Social Learning and Clinical Psychology*. Englewood Cliffs, N. J.: Prentice-Hall, 1954.

Thorne, Frederick, "Directive and Eclectic Personality Counseling." From James L. McCary, and Daniel E. Sheer, *Six Approaches to Psychotherapy*. New York: Dryden, 1955.

———, *Principles of Personality Counseling*. Brandon, Vt.: Journal of Clinical Psychology, 1950.

CHAPTER 9

Group Psychotherapy

Group psychotherapy was apparently first practiced with patients suffering from pulmonary tuberculosis by a Boston internist, Dr. Joseph H. Pratt, in 1905. One of the first applications of the group technique with psychoneurotics was by a minister (who later became a psychiatrist), L. Cody Marsh, in 1909. Psychodrama, a form of group therapy, was originated in 1911 by J. L. Moreno.

Soon after World War I, Dr. E. W. Lazell began experimental work in group procedures with schizophrenics in St. Elizabeth's Hospital in Washington, D. C. He later carried on this work in the Veterans Administration. The more psychoanalytically oriented type of group therapy began about 1930, grew fairly rapidly during the later thirties, and, along with many other group therapy orientations, mushroomed during and following World War II.

Today practically every type of individual therapy system has had some of its followers turn their attention to psychotherapeutic work with groups. While we can by no means sample all of the wide varieties of group therapy, we shall try to give some attention to most of the major approaches.

A. PSYCHODRAMA AND RELATED TECHNIQUES

J. L. Moreno first began to experiment with group therapeutic techniques with children in Vienna and was one of the early users of various group methods in the United States. The aim of group psychotherapy as conceived by Moreno is the integration of the patient's self against the uncontrolled forces around him. This is done by exploring his immediate environment by a process Moreno calls sociometric analysis and by helping the patient to understand and handle the environmental forces thus revealed. Free and spontaneous interaction is important in this type of group therapy. This includes relations among patients, between patients and therapists, and among therapists (usually more than one is present).

Chief therapist, auxiliary therapists, and patients are all equals in the therapeutic group as Moreno defines it. He feels that the group composition should resemble as nearly as possible a cross-section of the community in age, sex, ethnic characteristics, etc. The therapist has the therapeutic productivity and stability of the group as his main concern, but he also needs to consider himself as an equal patient, according to Moreno.

The interactional type of group psychotherapy was based on spontaneous interaction among members of the group assisted by a therapist, and psychodrama (linked with group psychotherapy by Moreno from 1936 onward) added the acting-out principle. Moreno and his followers consider psychodrama the depth therapy of the group and contend that "therapeutic acting out" in a controlled environment is both a preventive and curative measure against "irrational acting-out" in life itself.

In the course of interactional group sessions, a member of the group may experience an emotional problem of an intensity for which words seem insufficient. He has an urge to act out the situation, and, in psychodramatically oriented group therapy, a stage or specially designated area is provided for him to do so. One or another member of the group (which may be one of the therapists) may become involved in a counter-role and step upon the stage to co-act with the first patient. Others may or may not join in.

Many psychodramatic techniques have been developed through the years. Rules for their procedure are adapted as the group situation dictates and are not rigidly followed. Sometimes the main focus is on the group and sometimes it shifts to individual members of the group. One frequently helpful method for an individual to gain a new perspective of himself and his adjustment is what is called *role reversal:* A becomes B, and B becomes A, in an acting-out situation.

Another technique is that of the double: an auxiliary therapist, for example, joins Mr. X on the stage and plays the role of Mr. X, too. The double is useful in helping the patient to produce new hypotheses for avenues of further understanding. A variation of the double technique is what is called the mirror method. Here another group member plays Mr. X's role while Mr. X watches.

The foregoing are only a few samples of the psychodramatic devices that Moreno and others have developed. The chief value of psychodrama, according to its proponents, is that it takes place in a setting which approximates most closely the problem-producing situations of life. As problems appear, they are dealt with on the spot, and the solutions are extended to significant people and situations of the outer world. Psychodramatists contend that irrational and compulsive patterns are more readily seen and treated, in the situation which involves action rather than just conversation. Distortions of reality by the patients become quickly apparent and can be dealt with in the interpersonal relationships in which they arise. Thus, it is held, psychodrama goes beyond the theoretical insight characteristic of other forms of therapy and provides corrective emotional experience.

B. ANALYTIC GROUP THERAPY

The early work in group therapy by Dr. Lazell at St. Elizabeth's Hospital was undertaken from a psychoanalytic point of view in part, but tended to develop later along lines of inspirational exhortation. Pioneer work of a more clear-cut psychoanalytic variety was undertaken in the mid-thirties by Wender and Schilder. The former stressed insight, patient to patient transference, catharsis, and group interaction as the main factors of the group therapy process. Schilder extensively utilized the method of free association with groups of four to six patients, who were also being seen in individual analysis. The most extensive exploration of the psychoanalytic approach to group psychotherapy has been by S. R. Slavson, founding president of the American Group Psychotherapy Association and editor of that organization's *International Journal of Group Psychotherapy*.

Slavson has emphasized the importance of the selection of group members on such bases as clinical symptomatology, motivation for treatment, and intelligence. He, like Moreno, stresses spontaneity and feels that the major advantage of the group is that it permits the acting out of instinctual drives, which is facilitated by the stimulating effect of the group situation. Unlike Moreno, however, Slavson feels that it is the individual and not the group that should always be the focus of the therapist's attention. The group to Slavson is unimportant in itself and is simply a means for speeding up individual therapy. Catharsis, insight, transference relationships, reality testing, etc., are dynamic features of the analytic group situation, similar to, but not identical with, those found in individual therapy. In transference, there is what Slavson has called "target multiplicity": that is, the patient can displace feelings not only to the therapist, but to other patients, who often serve as sibling substitutes.

The ultimate aim of analytic group therapy, like individual psychoanalysis, is the facilitation of the fullest possible communication of unconscious material. In this process of making the patient more aware of his own unconscious, the group therapist has his difficulties increased greatly in one sense by having a complex network of transferences to analyze and interpret. In another sense, however, his task is reduced by the greater possibility of demonstrating and interpreting to the patient the unreality of his transference reaction in the group situation, where the patient can observe the differing transference reactions of his fellow group members. In addition, since each patient's transference reactions are distributed among members of the group, the analyst does not need to deal with the full force of transference on him personally as in individual psychoanalysis.

Some psychoanalysts who are inexperienced in group psychotherapy have questioned whether patients would achieve in the group setting the degree of self-exposure and free association which reveal deep unconscious conflicts. Experienced group analysts, like Slavson, contend that self-exposure can be even greater in the group, where the patient has the support and the example of self-revealing fellow patients. Although various types of resistances are encountered in the psychoanalytically oriented group (just as in the individual setting), experienced group therapists hold that they are often more readily overcome. It is believed that in an effectively operating group, the attitudes of fellow members often convince a resistive patient that his repressed feelings are not only acceptable, but that he will help the group and himself gain status and achieve further understanding by revealing them.

Psychoanalytically oriented group psychotherapists differ among themselves in some of their approaches. In general, however, they discourage group meetings held without the therapist (a pattern followed among some non-analytic therapists) or patient socialization outside the group sessions. Some analysts conduct individual therapy with the same patients they are seeing in the group, some refer group members to other analysts for individual therapy, and some hold that the group therapeutic procedures are sufficient without individual therapeutic supplementation. While new patients are frequently introduced into a group early in the history of that particular group, such a procedure is usually believed to be disruptive after a group has been long established.

The application of psychoanalysis to the field of group therapy is still quite new and fluid. It is probably safe to say that practically any group therapeutic procedure that the reader can imagine, as well as many he cannot imagine, has by now been practiced and reported in the literature by at least one psychoanalytically-oriented group therapist.

C. GROUP-CENTERED THERAPY

This system of group psychotherapy is the application of the client-centered therapeutic theories and techniques (see Chapter 6) to the group setting. It is believed that each member of a group needs to find the same feeling of acceptance from other group members, as the client finds from the therapist in individual therapy. The genuine expression of such feeling of acceptance by the group therapist, it is contended, spreads contagiously through the group, but it may take some time for it to do so. When it happens, however, it has more beneficial effects than acceptance by the therapist alone, for it is a more potent experience, according to the Rogersians, to be understood and accepted by several people who are honestly sharing their feelings in a joint enterprise than simply by a professionally understanding therapist.

As a general procedure, prospective group members are interviewed by the therapist prior to the first meeting of the group. At this time the therapist tries to learn something about the person's problems, to describe the way groups operate, to give him an opportunity to decide whether or not he wants to join a group, and to enable the therapist and the prospective member to develop some mutual feelings of security.

Groups are usually made up of about six clients and the therapist with no visitors permitted and no additions to the group after the first meeting. Although special groups are occasionally set up (such as for engaged or married couples), most groups are formed along such broadly selective lines as similarity of age (adults, children, adolescents), and degree of neurosis (there are of course separate groups for psychotics).

There is considerable flexibility regarding frequency and length of meetings for any particular group. The decision as to how often and how long to meet is usually left to the group, but once a pattern is set, it is usually adhered to. The most frequent pattern appears to be two meetings per week of about one hour's duration each, and the total number of meetings per group has tended to average about twenty.

As the reader of the client-centered point of view would assume, the therapist in group-centered therapy does not have prepared material for discussion by the group. The members are free to bring forth for discussion any problems they deem significant. As in individual therapy, the therapist's main role is not active interpretation, but acceptance, reflection, and clarification of attitudes and feelings presented in the group. The therapist is not strictly passive, however, for he intervenes in case he believes that one or more members of the group are blocking or threatening the free expression of feelings by any other member of the group.

The therapeutic role in group-centered therapy often falls to other members of the group than the therapist. Studies made by the client-centered school seem to indicate that in later sessions, group members become adept at assuming the therapeutic role for fellow members. That is to say, they seem to become more permissive and accepting and less inclined to be interpretive, evaluative, and critical. They are thus able more adequately to function in a way that assists other group members to explore their own feelings further.

One of the advantages of group-centered over individual client-centered therapy, according to its proponents, is the immediate opportunity it affords the group member to test the effectiveness of his ability to relate to people and to improve his skills in interpersonal relations. It provides the patient with many relationships rather than simply the one with the therapist. It seems likely (the Rogersians here agree with the Sullivanians) that the most important changes in personality can be worked out only in meaningful interpersonal relations, and the group has the advantage of providing many more opportunities for such interaction than individual therapy.

In general, the group-centered therapist needs qualities similar to the individual therapist. He must possess such qualities as unconditional positive regard for members of the group, empathic understanding of the feelings of group members and confidence in their ability to be responsible for themselves, with the ability to restrain on his part any tendency to intervene on the assumption that his point of view of the situation is superior. Experience in individual client-centered therapy is believed to be the best preparation for a leader of group-centered therapy.

D. FAMILY THERAPY

A somewhat new approach in psychotherapy is to consider the family, rather than the individual, as the unit in which emotional illness occurs and therefore the unit toward which treatment needs to be directed. There have been various independent therapeutic attempts at family treatment, one of which is that of C. F. Midelfort, a Wisconsin psychiatrist.

Midelfort's point of view is that there tend to be balancing and opposing psychopathologies within a family. A patient with obsessive-compulsive neurosis, for example, is likely to have a family in which some members will have patterns similar to his and other members will have impulsive, acting-out behavior. The latter family members are expressing directly what the obsessive-compulsives are concealing and controlling by their rigidity. Husband and wife, Midelfort states, often show these opposite traits, and their children as well. If the first child is obsessive-compulsive, the second will be like the other parent (impulsive). The third child is likely to be more like the first than the second, and so on in a balancing-opposing pattern.

Each group in a family such as the foregoing is a threat to the other, and one of the roles of the therapist is to remove this threat and help each to become more like the other. In the example presented, the obsessive-compulsive family members are encouraged to feel safe about expressing their impulses more spontaneously, and the impulsive members are helped to exercise more strict controls. A better balance can thus be achieved, and many symptoms can be eliminated. The reason the family cannot do this without therapeutic help is that each group provokes an exaggeration of the existing reaction in the other as a defense against becoming like the other.

In interviews he conducts with families of the type we have described, Midelfort gives assurance and permission for each type of behavior pattern. First he supports the obsessive-compulsive to be the way he is. The impulsive spouse is then encouraged to admit obsessive-compulsive traits within himself. As this formerly very impulsive spouse becomes more obsessive-compulsive (by releasing such tendencies unconsciously there, but previously repressed), the obsessive-compulsive patient can relax and become aware and accepting of his own impulsiveness. The new balance thus established is of less opposing extremes, and the intrapsychic and intrafamily conflict potentials are considerably reduced.

Midelfort takes comparable approaches to the foregoing in dealing with other types of mental illness. The therapist's role, as he sees it, is to analyze the kinds of dynamic interactional patterns in operation in a family, to determine how the therapist can break the circular processes that are handicapping and defeating family members, and to utilize the unconscious accompaniments of existing roles to work out an equilibrium less threatening to each family member.

Individual therapy is used conjunctively with family therapy by Midelfort. He believes, however, that the exclusive use of the former causes a wider gap to form between the patient and his family and may lead to the breaking up of family life. By also using the family therapy technique of bringing the family and patient together in interviews with the therapist, Midelfort believes the family unity can be strengthened. In the family interview, he states, there is a greater objectivity achieved, which leads the family out of its subjective, pathological interactions. The therapist can demonstrate simultaneously for family members an objective and united approach to their problem situations.

Midelfort contends that the main goal of individual therapy is the overcoming of the patient's unconscious and subjective blocks against group activity. When such blocks are sufficiently removed or reduced, the patient then needs to learn to make real and objective those activities that satisfy his social needs. This he can learn to do through group participation. Since the group to which the patient most urgently needs to learn to relate with less disturbance and greater effectiveness is his own family, and since usually the other members are themselves in need of education in more effective interpersonal functioning, family therapy is often the most desirable form of group therapy.

E. OTHER ORIENTATIONS

A psychologist, George R. Bach, has made a serious effort to combine the field theory of Kurt Lewin (essentially Gestalt psychology applied to the study of groups and termed "group dynamics") with a psychoanalytic orientation in developing his system of group psychotherapy. He feels that many of the approaches to group psychotherapy have been simply the application of individual therapeutic techniques without thorough knowledge of the structure and function of groups themselves. While we cannot summarize the intricate interweavings of psychoanalytic and group dynamic theories and practices made by Bach, we shall point out a few of his practical suggestions regarding the operations of group psychotherapy.

Five types of patients, Bach believes, should be excluded from groups: those with insufficient reality contact (psychotics), the cultural deviants (homosexual or criminal, who function best in groups that are composed of individuals with similar symptoms), the extremely dominant and monopolistic personalities, the psychopathically defensive and impulsive, and those with acute environmental crises (recent divorce, death of a child, etc.). Certain types of persons may be acceptable in one group and not another, according to Bach. One group, for example, may have an opening for an aggressive male, while such an individual would be quite disruptive in another group. Bach also cautions against too great heterogeneity of backgrounds (religion, age, etc.), but feels that broadly representative social experiences should be included as much as possible. The range of intelligence should not be too great for ready communication.

Bach holds that the group leader should play the following procedural roles: (1) reflection of group-originated communications with some simplification and facilitation of understandability when needed; (2) some interpretation of group emotions linked with occasional summaries; (3) occasional functioning as an expert to familiarize the group with techniques that may be utilized (such as dream association, psychodrama, and projective drawing). The therapist should also encourage members of the group to act on the principle that while there are no secrets inside the group, all group activities should be kept confidential. In practice this means that everything anybody says, thinks, or does which involves another member of the group is open to discussion in the group, but that each member will feel secure about his behaviors not being a topic of discussion by outsiders.

The group's goal, as Bach sees it, is free communication on a non-defensive, personal, and emotional basis. He feels that the group leader cannot push the group in its progress, but can merely act as a facilitator or catalyst. In general, each member will obtain benefit to the degree of his own efforts. Members who communicate to the group their feelings, association, and perceptions with openness and consistency will, in the long run, find the group a therapeutically effective medium.

Hubert S. Coffey and associates have taken a Sullivanian approach to the study of group therapy. They have made the specific assumption that the problems of the emotionally disturbed person lie in the conflict between the patient's conception of himself and what he communicates to others. This often amounts to the difference between the patient's conscious and unconscious social roles, and the group therapeutic situation, according to Coffey, offers him the best opportunity (if properly conducted) to see these two sets of roles in relation to each other.

Coffey and associates have distinguished three phases of group development: (1) the period of defensiveness and resistance, in which the patients act out the conflicts between conscious and unconscious roles that have caused them difficulty in their other interpersonal relations. In this first phase, the role of the therapist is largely one of allowing free description of their views of themselves and their problems by group members. (2) The next phase is one referred to as that of confiding. In this period much emphasis is given to discussion of dreams, fantasies, early experiences, and less anxiety is shown regarding maintenance of conscious social roles. The therapist in this phase mainly supports testing out of unconscious roles and revelation of their possible sources and provides supporting and clarifying data from the first period of the group's development. A close interpersonal bond tends to develop in this second phase of the group. (3) The last period is referred to as the integrative-prospective. Interpretations from both therapist and group members become more integrative and extensive. Comprehensive summaries for each group member are allowed for in the sessions of this third stage (the last seven of a total of 24 sessions). If the therapy has been successful, the patient now sees the conflict between his conscious and unconscious roles, becomes aware of his rigid social techniques, and, with the group's help, develops new views of himself and his relations with others.

A didactic or pedagogical approach to group therapy has been developed by J. W. Klapman and others. In this approach the lecture material is the main basis of organization and orientation. A series of lectures is presented on such topics as the nature of the common attitudes toward mental illness, types of neurotic conflict, relationship of the mentally ill person to society and vice versa, mechanisms of defense, forms of resistance to therapy, spontaneous resurgence to mental health, and so on. Along with the lectures, readings are assigned and discussed, autobiographies are written and presented, controversial subjects are debated, special readings are assigned to group members for oral presentation to the group, etc. In short, as the term didactic group therapy implies, these are classes in mental health for the mentally ill.

The last type of group psychotherapy that we shall mention is one developed in a state hospital. Its goals are to help patients to gain realistic perspectives regarding their problems and to develop confidence in themselves and in the helping attitudes of others in working out satisfactory solutions to their problems. The therapy, referred to as round-table psychotherapy, is based on the premise that a patient will gain better self-understanding by trying to understand and help others.

Round-table therapy is set up in such a way that a panel of seven patients discuss the problems of one of the seven in front of an audience of eighteen (the remainder of the patients on the ward). The therapist becomes the eighth, but relatively inactive, member of the panel. The therapist has a pre-panel discussion, however, with each of the seven participants. The procedure is one of encouraging the six patients to induce the seventh to discuss his problems freely and to help him solve these problems. The panel is also given considerable authority in making recommendations regarding the treatment of the patient whose problems are discussed.

Variations in the foregoing procedures have been undertaken in other hospitals. Increasingly group therapeutic techniques of various types are employed in hospitals to improve the effectiveness of individual therapy (of both the psychological and medical varieties) and raise the morale and esprit de corps of the hospital patients and staff.

Summary

Group psychotherapies of various kinds have developed rapidly since World War II. The types dealt with in this chapter are psychodrama, analytic group therapy, group-centered therapy, family therapy, the orientations of Bach and Coffey, the didactic approach, and round-table psychotherapy.

The aim of group psychotherapy, as conceived by Moreno, is the integration of the patient's self against the uncontrolled forces around him. He feels free and spontaneous interaction is important in achieving this goal. The "depth" type of such interactional group therapy, according to Moreno, is therapeutic acting out, called psychodrama.

The psychoanalytic point of view has been applied to group psychotherapy by many workers, most notable of whom is Slavson. Catharsis, insight, transference relationships, reality testing, and the like are dynamic features of the analytic group situation, similar to those found in individual analysis. Both special difficulties and special aids are found in group analytic, as compared with individual analytic, therapy. The ultimate aim of the two is the same, however: the facilitation of the fullest possible communication of unconscious material.

Group-centered therapy is the application of the Rogersian approach to group psychotherapy. Feelings of acceptance are stressed in group-centered as in individual client-centered therapy. While difficulties are sometimes encountered in helping each member of the group to be positively accepting of every other member, the effect, when achieved, is considered even more valuable than such acceptance by the therapist in individual therapy. One of the advantages of group-centered over individual client-centered therapy, according to its exponents, is the immediate opportunity it affords the group member to test the effectiveness of his ability to relate to people and to improve his skills in interpersonal relations.

The family is the group treated in a type of group psychotherapy developed by Midelfort. His point of view is that there tend to be balancing and opposing psychopathologies within a family. By treating the whole family, instead of just an individual family member, Midelfort believes he can more effectively help each member to better mental health by bringing about a more realistic, less repressed equilibrium in family interactions.

Bach has combined the field theory of Kurt Lewin with the psychoanalytic orientation in his form of group psychotherapy. The group goal, as Bach sees it, is free communication on a nondefensive, personal, and emotional basis. The group leader can facilitate the group's reaching this goal by various techniques Bach discusses.

Coffey and associates have made an application of some of Sullivan's ideas to group therapy. They assume that the problems of the emotionally disturbed person lie in the conflict between the patient's conception of himself and what he communicates to others. The main function of group therapy is to help the patient to see his unconsciously operating social roles.

In didactic or pedagogical group therapy the stress is placed on communicating mentally healthful concepts to members of the group through lectures, readings, symposia, special reports, and other educational devices. Round-table psychotherapy is a method developed in a mental hospital whereby a panel of patients discuss the problems of a fellow patient, in the presence of a therapist.

Selected Readings

Bach, George R., *Intensive Group Psychotherapy*. New York: Ronald, 1954.

Coffey, Hubert S. "Group Psychotherapy." From L. A. Pennington, and I. A. Berg, *An Introduction to Clinical Psychology*, 2nd ed. New York: Ronald, 1954.

Hobbs, Nicholas, "Group-Centered Psychotherapy." In Carl R. Rogers, *Client-Centered Therapy*. New York: Houghton, 1951.

Klapman, J. W., *Group Psychotherapy: Theory and Practice*. New York: Grune, 1946.

Midelfort, C. F., *The Family in Psychotherapy*. New York: McGraw, 1957.

Moreno, J. L., *Psychodrama*. New York: Beacon, 1946.

Powdermaker, Florence B., and J. D. Frank, *Group Psychotherapy*. Cambridge, Mass.: Harvard, 1953.

Slavson, S. R., *Analytic Group Psychotherapy*. New York: Columbia, 1950.

CHAPTER **10**

Critique and Overview

In this final chapter, our difficult task is to try to ascertain, in as clear and objective a manner as possible, what the various systems of psychotherapy each have to offer.

Let us make a broad division of the various schools into two main categories: A. the emotionally oriented, or affective, therapies and B. the intellectually oriented, or cognitive, therapies. Group A constitutes the great bulk of psychotherapeutic systems: all types of psychoanalysis, with the exception of Adler's individual psychology (which is discussed as a form of psychoanalysis more for historical than content purposes), client-centered therapy, Gestalt therapy, hypnotherapy, experiential therapy, conditioned reflex therapy, therapy by reciprocal inhibition and all of the group psychotherapies except didactic group therapy. At times the dynamic culturalists (especially Sullivan and Fromm) veer in the cognitive direction, but most of their therapeutic efforts, like those of the rest of Group A, are directed toward what may be called emotional reconditioning.

Group B may be considered therapeutic nonconformists. The psychobiologic therapists belong primarily in this group, even though they pay some token respect to certain psychoanalytic techniques and theories. Adlerians, who have frankly developed what they refer to as an educational type of therapy, may be considered cognitive therapists. The entire group in Chapter 8 are mainly oriented toward intellectual reconditioning. And that, with the addition of the already mentioned didactic group therapists, is the whole of Group B. None of the therapists in this group have an extensive following.

It would seem, therefore, that Group B is swimming against the therapeutic current, and so it is in some ways. Yet actually the affective vs. cognitive issue is not so simple as it at first appears. Not only have the dynamic culturalists brought increasing emphasis on ego instead of id in deviant psychoanalytic circles, but even the classical analytic group has in practice spent more and more of its time and attention in analysis of the ego defenses, rather than prolonged unwinding of the id impulses. This is a trend in the direction of greater attention to the cognitive, the executive, the less deeply unconscious (if not actually conscious) aspects of the personality.

The client-centered therapists are deep within the affective division of therapy. They speak almost exclusively of feelings, emotional experience, acceptance, emotional safety, love, positive regard, empathy, and similar topics of affect. The Rogersians are actually relying, in final analysis, on the ability of the patient to emerge from the warm, accepting atmosphere of therapy with more rational, logical, efficient, realistic ego structure. They feel that the cognitive aspects of the personality can function adequately once the emotional blocks are dissolved by the accepting therapeutic environment. Although the Rogersians conduct much rationally oriented research, the weight of the influence of their therapeutic system strikes this writer as being in the reactionary tradition of mysticism and art rather than in the direction of advancing rationality and science.

The experiential therapy of Whitaker and Malone, though startlingly "radical" in some of its techniques (such as the occasional use of aggression and therapeutic sleeping), is even more reactionary in its impact, for it advocates a return to the early psychoanalytic emphasis on the deep unconscious forces (the id impulses). These therapists direct their whole effort toward removing the rational, cognitive ego functions from the treatment situation and concentrating on primary processes of communication: fantasy relationships between therapist's id and patient's id. Such activities by their very nature tend to rule out the application of the rational tools of science. We must, however, acknowledge a further factor. It is quite apparent that much of the work undertaken by Whitaker and Malone is with very sick persons, for the most part psychotics. A rational, realistic approach is considerably less effective with a person who has renounced rationality and has escaped from reality than with a neurotic who is simply exhibiting various self-defeating patterns of reality. Understood in this sense, experiential therapy may be a necessary therapeutic departure from rationality for the purpose of meeting and helping the psychotic in his own world of unreality.

The Rogersians, on the other hand, are dealing primarily with mildly disturbed patients, and their rejection of a cognitive approach to their patients' needs to be understood in another frame of reference.

Client-centered therapy, it seems to me, is most clearly and objectively perceived as a historical correction. Rogers developed his emphasis on permissiveness as a reaction to a kind of totalitarianism which had developed in the field of psychotherapy in the late thirties. The Freudians in the twenties and early thirties were the unrecognized minority in the psychiatric fraternity. By the late thirties they had not only won their battle for legitimate recognition among psychiatrists and the general public, but were experiencing a wave of high prestige. Psychoanalysis was being much sought after as a kind of general cure-all for social, as well as personal, problems. As is true of many minorities who newly acquire power, arrogant and dictatorial attitudes were not uncommon among psychoanalytically trained psychiatrists. These attitudes are still to be encountered, but there is a growing realistic humility today regarding the limitations of both the techniques and theories of psychoanalysis among many analysts.

This atmosphere of totalitarianism in psychotherapy in the thirties was further strengthened by the attitudes of psychiatric social workers who came to function in ancillary roles to psychiatrists in clinics, hospitals, and private and public agencies. The service concept was so effectively drilled into most social workers of at least that generation that most of them functioned in devoted, unquestioning servitude (a servitude which was further enhanced by the fact that most psychiatrists were men and most social workers were women). The psychoanalyst's utterance was the not-to-be-disputed word of authority.

It required an intelligent, emotionally independent, male psychologist, free of any feeling of need to be beholden to the psychiatric group or the psychoanalytic sub-group, to lead a successful rebellion against the father figure of the psychoanalyst. The need for such a psychologist was filled by Carl Rogers, and the way he rebelled was naturally structured by his personal and professional predispositions.

His method can be fairly compared to the route taken by Ghandi and his followers in achieving Indian independence of the British. Like Ghandi, Rogers brought about no head-on clash of bristling authority with bristling counter-authority. He quietly emulated Ghandi by non-violently resisting the dictates of authority. He demonstrated in theory, in practice, and in research that people can be just as effectively helped without the complicated psychoanalytic superstructure of technique and mythology of theory. His non-violent rebellion gathered momentum by being joined not only by many other psychologists, but by dissatisfied elements in other professions: ministers, educators, sociologists, social workers, and even a few psychiatrists. As we discussed early in Chapter 6, part of the strength of the client-centered approach was drawn from its appeal to factors deep within the American culture.

The psychotherapeutic revolutionary war would seem to have been won by the rebels. Psychologists and others than psychiatrists and psychoanalysts are increasingly practicing psychotherapy of their own individual choosing.

But some of the post-independence problems of psychotherapy seem resistive to solution by the methods of the revolution. Just as the Indians have found that passive non-resistance does not solve difficulties that they have had to face since the departure of the British, the realistic psychotherapist must admit that not all therapeutic problems respond to emotional permissiveness in the clinical setting.

What Rogers has recently suggested as the necessary and sufficient conditions for psychotherapeutic personality change (see the latter part of Chapter 6) may be what he has labeled them for some *slightly* disturbed patients. Such conditions may even be necessary and sufficient for some moderately to severely disturbed patients whose main problem has been a feeling of being unloved and unaccepted. But this writer shares the point of view of other non-Rogersian clinicians that there are many quite disturbed patients for whom unconditional positive regard and empathic understanding, however well communicated, are insufficient to effect psychotherapeutic personality change. While awaiting the research for which Rogers calls to test these and other therapeutic hypotheses, many clinicians join Thorne (see Chapter 8) in emphasizing the need of many patients for therapeutic direction, diagnosis, and recovery plans based increasingly on the tools of rationality.

In a sense, the client-centered therapeutic atmosphere is the best possible recapture of the uterine environment for the patient. Although Rogers admits his partial dependence on Otto Rank, it is doubtful if he would approve our harking back to the heart of Rankian theory: emotional disturbance mainly traceable to the birth trauma. But the patient who experiences an approximation of unconditional positive regard for and empathic understanding of all his characteristics is getting the closest he will ever get in adult life to the completely satisfying, undemanding environment of prenatal life. To a considerable degree (but perhaps not always to what sounds like an overly seductive, Rogersian degree), acceptance and reassurance may be considered helpful *pre*-conditions to the serious, often cognitive, sometimes directive business which then needs to follow, as many non-Rogersian therapists would see it. This "further business" of therapy is the help needed by an individual who has seriously failed to adapt himself to life as an adult. A brief sojourn in the womblike atmosphere of Rogersian therapy may give such a person the recuperative strength he needs to face the job of learning how to handle the problems of the very unwomblike, non-therapeutic world of adult reality. But many such persons need direct guidance, specific education, in how to utilize their energies in effective, rational, realistic adaptation to interpersonal actualities. Thus it seems, at least, to a non-Rogersian.

What are the most valuable forms of direct guidance and specific education? Much would seem to depend upon specific diagnosis in each instance. But it must be admitted that the best of current psychological and psychiatric diagnostic methods, from Sullivanian analysis of early interpersonal acculturation through psychometric tests to Freudian dream interpretation via free association, are crude, largely unvalidated, and often unreliable tools. This brings us back to the undeniable realization that much more research is needed. But we cannot wait for the results of research in order to proceed to meet the psychotherapeutic needs of many members of our society. Meantime, a number of rational, though not yet scientifically established, guides can be explored by therapists who are willing to experiment with some unfamiliar approaches (a notable example of which is the rational reconditioning process suggested by Albert Ellis).

Such experimentation calls for less rigid adherence to any particular system of psychotherapy, and one wonders if the time has not arrived for greater emphasis on eclecticism, synthesis, flexibility in the use of differing therapeutic techniques. The dogmatic schools of psychotherapy were perhaps historically necessary for various desirable changes of public and professional climate (of which the Rogerian revolution was simply the most recent). It seems likely now, however, that further progress is more blocked than enhanced by clinging to psychotherapeutic "religions." There are two characteristics of rigid systemists: (1) their closed minds about points of view and outright facts which fail to fit their system and (2) their manifestation of what the psychoanalysts call "reaction formations." Let us illustrate these two assertions.

First, we have the current ruling class in psychotherapy: the Freudians. Although, as indicated earlier, humility is beginning to become a part of their personalities, there is still a persisting tendency among many in this group to believe they have the *only* valid answers to the nature of the human psyche and the treatment of psychic disorders. The more rigid and fanatic of the Freudians react roughly in the fashion of religious fundamentalists. Tell a fundamentalist that you think many Biblical stories are to be viewed as allegories and myths, and he has had enough of you. Tell a fundamentalist Freudian that you question the efficiency of free association, the universality of the Oedipus complex or the three stages of infantile sexuality, and his reaction is much the same. He does not care what brand of the devil you have assumed—dynamic culturalist, client-centered therapist, Adlerian, Jungian, or psychobiologist—he knows that your understanding of human behavior is *superficial* (the Freudian equivalent of Satanic) and that your resistance to Freudian doctrine is a manifestation of your own ego defenses against psychosexual truth. Such defensiveness, such repression of the point of view of the "enemy," would indicate in the Freudians, by their own analytical theories, feelings of insecurity. For the patient to admit hate, as well as love, for a parent, is an intolerable ego threat. For an orthodox Freudian to admit doubt in, as well as faith and acceptance of, classical psychoanalytic theory, may be a similarly intolerable ego threat. Such unswerving Freudian faith is suspiciously symptomatic of a reaction formation.

Closed minds and reaction formations are equally evident in fanatics of other persuasions. The psychoanalysis-hating Salter, the Freud-biting Horney, the Freud-repressing Sullivan, the Freud-rejecting Adler and Jung (and those who orthodoxly follow these and other therapeutic messiahs) show an unwillingness to listen objectively and to consider the possible merit of opposing positions. Because of their permissive exterior, such dogmatism is, though present, less evident, in the Rogersians. They are quite fearful of and incapable of dealing adequately with strong, opposing points of view and with authoritarian figures because of their anxiety about their own repressed tendencies toward dictatorial behavior. A Salter who violently overthrows *all* Freudian procedures and theories as utter nonsense must be, by the hypothesis of reaction formation, fighting down some pro-analytic tendencies inside himself that frighten him. The client-centered therapist who pushes down *all* therapist direction, *all* diagnosis, *all* functions of the therapist other than exudence of positive regard and empathy for the omnipotent client, must, by this same hypothesis, be repressing strong authoritarian impulses in himself that he fears and doubts that he can handle. In fairness, it should be pointed out that those therapists who emphatically reject everything the Rogersians have to offer are undoubtedly afraid of soft, accepting, love-giving tendencies in *their* repressed psyches.

While we await research findings (and for definitively helpful results, it is bound to be a long wait), it would appear that many therapists and their patients are likely to profit from a flexible repertoire of therapeutic techniques, rather than from a rigid adherence to a single system of psychotherapy. It is encouraging to observe a growing trend of eclecticism among therapists of many persuasions. (This trend is being fought, however, by some classical analysts, some Rogersians, and others.)

Phillips and Ellis are two cognitively oriented therapists whose writings to date in support of assertion-structured therapy and rational psychotherapy, respectively, give the appearance of anti-eclecticism. It is possible, however, that at least part of their denunciation of other systems is designed to attract greater attention to their own genuine contributions. Both have made significant eclectic contributions prior to the development of their own therapeutic systems, and there is every reason to believe they will do so in the future. Meantime, their systems of psychotherapy serve as an effective challenge to psychoanalysts, client-centered therapists, and others that concentrate largely on emotional reconditioning.

Wolpe brings, in some ways, an even stronger challenge to the theoretical superstructures and the elaborate techniques of many of the therapies in both groups A and B. While it seems likely at this point that his system is based on an oversimplification of human behavior, emotional disturbance, and the therapeutic process, new experimental testing of therapy will be stimulated by his theories and techniques.

The coolest eclectics and rationalists to date in this warm, emotional springtime of psychotherapy would seem to be the learning theory therapists, the psychobiologists, and Thorne. The latter two are eclectics in the full sense of the term, and their major influence in the whole field has been that of pointing out neglected techniques and theories of aid in treating all types of disturbed persons. The learning theory therapists have made their main emphasis that of clearing away mysticism from many varieties of approaches and offering ways of testing by future research many of the hypotheses about human personality, its pathological developments, and methods of treating these pathologies (to this point, however, their actual research production falls considerably below that of Rogers and associates). Thorne and the psychobiologists have likewise underlined reliance on the products of science in the training and functioning of therapists.

The general semanticists have made a contribution which has begun to be absorbed into the general therapeutic stream: namely, the focus of much more careful attention on the whole communicative process, both inside and outside the treatment setting. Much more needs to be learned here, but even now the therapist can function more effectively (whatever other techniques he uses or theories he holds) by devoting a considerable portion of his perceptive skills to his and the patient's transmission of meaning.

The experiments or exercises offered by the Gestaltists need to be explored much more carefully by therapists of many differing points of view. Without necessarily holding to all of the theories of Perls and his associates, the eclectic therapist may find here a technique for rendering more effective the attitude change of some patients.

Hypnosis is being re-explored in a number of therapeutic settings. Caution is needed here, as Wolberg has pointed out, because of the magical aura associated with the technique in the minds of many people. As a tool to be selectively employed, however, hypnosis is part of the legitimate equipment of the skilled therapist.

While Whitaker and Malone may in a sense lead us further away from a rational, scientific approach to psychotherapy by their emphasis on id communication, their techniques have certainly had a healthful effect in challenging *any* rigid, dogmatic assumptions about what will or will not work in psychotherapy. Other imaginative and instructive techniques (including the use of multiple therapists, a method not discussed in our book) continue to emerge from the Atlanta psychiatric center. Future therapeutic developments must certainly take into account the experimental proceedings of Whitaker, Malone, and associates.

The simple technique outlined by Ellis of getting patients to understand the self-verbalized perpetuations of their negative emotions and to learn to substitute more rational and realistic thought which will (allegedly) produce neutral or positive emotional conditions needs much further investigation and therapeutic experimentation. Research which will pit the accepting, affective approach of Rogers, for example, against the directive, cognitive techniques of Ellis should prove valuable. It is encouraging to report that both Rogers and Ellis have independently indicated strong interest in such research.

The group psychotherapies not only offer new ways for helping patients to facilitate the development of greater insights into personality characteristics that they have tended to repress, dissociate, or disown, but also present a practice situation in which the patient can develop his skills in interpersonal relations. To this point, enthusiasm for systems and particular techniques have followed to some extent the route of individual psychotherapy. However, the group experience itself is destructive of dogmatism and rigidity in the therapist, and so a great deal of imaginative trial-and-accidental-success learning has tended to ensue. This has made some contribution to the flexibility of individual therapeutic practices. It is hoped that at least some of the future experimentation in group psychotherapy can develop along systematic research lines which encourage scientific reduplication.

What, then, of psychoanalysis? It seems indisputable that at this point in the development of psychotherapy many of the Freudian theories (especially with certain of the more moderate "corrections" of the dynamic culturalists) are still the best available for an over-all working hypothesis regarding the functioning of the human personality. The more thinking of Freud's critics draw heavily (as many of them admit) upon his insights even in the course of their criticisms. In the writer's opinion, the most sagacious eclectic therapists of at least this generation are likely to be theoretically, and to some extent technically, psychoanalytically oriented. Meantime, many of the psychoanalytic hypotheses can be reformulated (as some already have) in operational terms and tested, along with other hypotheses in large, co-ordinated research projects (still largely in a fantasy stage).

What is the common ground of all these therapies we have considered? How can people be helped by such divergent procedures as those of the classical analyst or the client-centered therapist, on the one hand, and those of the rational therapist or the assertion-structured therapist, on the other?

The following observations about common aspects of psychotherapy are in terms of *effects,* as distinguished from the techniques which were discussed in Chapter 1. They are presented in the form of assertions, but are to be considered tentative hypotheses to be tested by future research. Not all of these observations apply to all patients at all times with all forms of psychotherapy, nor are these common effects the totality of results of any particular system of therapy. They are simply current conceptions of frequently occurring results of the work of many therapists with many of the patients with whom they seem to have success.

First of all, weak egos (those of the patients) at least temporarily gain support from strong egos (those of the therapists). Stated differently, persons with initially low self-esteem gain in this area through intimate association with persons of generally high self-esteem. "*He* (the self-respecting therapist) likes and accepts and gives attention to and cares for and is concerned about *me.* I, therefore, must be better, more worthwhile, less hopeless, etc., than I had thought."

The first effect can be achieved in numerous ways. It can be done by a very non-directive method of largely listening, non-critically feeding back what the patient has said, showing infinite patience and acceptance. Or it can be done relatively impersonally behind the couch on which the patient rests, but with occasional interpretations which demonstrate that the analyst has been listening carefully and that the patient has a fascinating and complicated unconscious (otherwise, the patient feels, why would the analyst consider it worthwhile to spend three or four hours per week listening and interpreting?). Or it can be done by rational instruction, emotional reconditioning (including Wolpe's point of reciprocal inhibition), confirmation and disconfirmation, sharing of fantasy experiences, and consideration of alleged symbols of an alleged collective unconscious. Any of these methods and many others give the patient attention at the very minimum and often understanding, acceptance, and love. As with the child (and in any therapeutic system this is the role the patient at least temporarily takes), even punitive attention from the parent (therapist) brings the feeling that "I am at least worthy of this strong person's time and energy, and I am, hence, of some importance."

The second common effect of psychotherapy is that less rational and less reality-oriented persons (patients) at least temporarily learn more realistic ways of handling life problems from more rational and reality-oriented persons (therapists). They can be specifically told how better to deal with reality, or they can gradually come to imitate the examples set by the therapists over a period of time. But directly or indirectly they are taught (yes, *taught*—though this is a rejected word in many a therapist's vocabulary, the process goes on) by therapists how to behave less disturbedly in confronting their life activities.

Third, patients also learn (again, the methods may be very direct or very devious) that a lot of the things that they have fretted, stewed, or panicked over are not as important as they thought. (The observation that psychotherapy is the process whereby the unbland learn to be led by the bland into becoming bland has some truth in it.) In one way or another, successful therapy reduces anxiety by communicating to the patient that his concerns about what his neighbors think, his guilt feelings about not having been nice to his mother before she died, his worries about not being acceptable to the members of a social club, etc., are at best unnecessary and at worst idiotic. He is directly taught such things, or he indirectly comes to "catch on" to them by associating with a person who is quite bland about such matters.

Fourth, patients learn patience. One of the most frequent difficulties of persons with emotional immaturity and certain forms of emotional disturbance is a low tension capacity. The very process of going through the long and tedious process of therapy week after week, discussing the frequently recurring problems and hearing or otherwise sensing the same suggested ways of handling these difficulties, develops the person's tension capacity, his ability to be patient. Stated differently, patients gradually learn to be less childish, more adult. They learn to insist less on immediately satisfying goal-responses and to put up with tensions necessary to achieve long-term goals. They learn sometimes by instruction, sometimes by example —usually by both.

Fifth, patients learn new sets of myths (a "new faith"), which at least seem to be more scientific, more closely related to contemporary social reality, than their old sets of myths. The myths the patients adopt are their perceptions of the therapists' beliefs. Whether or not the therapists and the patients are aware of the myth-adopting process seems to have little effect on its efficiency. Therapists of a few of the systems (Ellis, Phillips, Salter, and the Adlerians, for several examples) would seem to be frank propagandists: they admit they are attempting to instill their systems of value in their patients. But others, including the most non-directive of the Rogersians and the most classically impersonal of the Freudians, have their patients as evidence that they, too, transmit their values. Patients even come to dream the kinds of dreams, in some instances, that they feel are most appreciated by their therapist.

Since it is very likely that even the most unrealistic myth system of a fairly healthy therapist will function more effectively (at least for a time) than the probably quite confused myth system the patient brought with him to therapy, improvement is likely to ensue from the change in values for the patient.

Sixth, patients gain perspective about their emotions and their interactional difficulties from talking about them and hearing the therapist talk about them. Such talk in itself tends to objectify fears, anxieties, feelings of inadequacy, and so on. The patient finds it gradually more difficult to react with intense fear to, say, open spaces, after all the angles of the nature and possible causes of his phobic fear have been discussed at length by the therapist and himself. Another patient who has always been late to appointments, who postpones other responsibilities, and lies late abed each morning begins to lose his neurotic satisfaction from such tactics of avoidance after he and the therapist have conversationally dealt with these and related factors at great length. The personal privacy, the hidden subjectivity, of various aspects of neurosis can be removed by talk alone (even if the talk is devoid of insight into causation and does nothing other than expose the problems to objective discussion), and sometimes the emotional disturbance loses its power with its privacy.

Seventh, by focusing so much attention on present anxieties while in therapy, patients are likely to find future anxieties less threatening. Not only have the old problems lost a lot of their ego-damaging punch (for such reasons as those discussed in the foregoing points), but new problems often seem weak, pale, and manageable in contrast to the former anxiety investments in the problems subjected to the tedious inspection of psychotherapy. "Nothing can throw me after I live through this" is a sometimes valid reaction of the patient in the process of therapy.

Patients often emerge from therapy with the feeling that the therapist is a part of them and, hence, life will never again be so lonely or so difficult. This intense emotional experience derives from the personal, intimate, problem-inspecting process with even a relatively cold and impersonal therapist. "He's there; he understands; he thinks I am worthwhile. I am not alone; I have some of his strength; I can handle whatever lies ahead."

The points we have just brought out are, we think, observable in psychotherapy as a whole. It should be understood, however, that some systems may more consistently and efficiently achieve these and other important effects. And some therapists, regardless of system affiliation or lack of same, achieve much better results than their colleagues. With any therapist and any system, such results as those we have discussed are by no means inevitable—failures seem at least as plentiful as successes.

Psychotherapy is, if we may now generalize from our list of common effects, a contemporary means for individuals with poorly functioning value systems to find the support of an apparently strong and successful person in learning a new value system and how to live more effectively thereby. None of these value systems learned in therapy may be considered totally satisfactory for meeting the problems of present-day social turbulence. They are varyingly successful stopgap measures for persons who no longer get sufficient ego strength and relationship support from such long-standing institutions (value systems) as the church, the school, marriage, and the family.

We use the term "stopgap measure" advisedly, for it seems quite evident that as the ever-brighter light of science increasingly penetrates psychotherapy, all the systems of this make-shift institution will reveal more fiction than fact, more myth than science. The day may not be too distant—with the advances of biochemistry, physiology, and biophysics, as well as psychology itself—that what we now call psychotherapy will relate to the scientific treatment and prevention of behavioral disorders as astrology now relates to astronomy.

While we look to that day, however, much work must be done with the present primitive tools of psychotherapy. Blunt instruments are surely rendered no sharper by rigidity, dogmatism, and fanatic adherence to a particular system. Young therapists in training should be encouraged to expose themselves to the full range of therapeutic theories and to experiment with the complete repertory of therapeutic techniques. Such therapists, in this period which is hopefully a prelude to more scientific procedures, are more likely, we firmly believe, to be helpful to a great number of patients than therapists conditioned in one theoretical orientation and its limited techniques.

But this is the outlook of an eclectic, and an eclectic is often less acceptable to fanatics than even fanatics of opposing persuasions. Scorning the wrath of the faithful of all systems of psychotherapy, we offer this book as an introduction to therapeutic eclecticism. We are saying, in effect, throughout: look around, reserve judgment for a while and then make it tentative, and experiment with many theories and techniques. Until science brings us definitive answers—if science does—let us try to avoid commitment to a rigid religion of psychotherapy. Let us learn from and constructively employ the arts of many therapies.

Glossary

Words italicized in the definitions are themselves defined in their alphabetical order.

acting out: performing in a new setting the *behavior* learned from and appropriate to another social situation.

active analytic psychotherapy: the term applied to the deviant form of *psychoanalysis* developed by Wilhelm Stekel (see Section B of Chapter 4).

affect: emotion, feeling, mood, feeling tone, temperament. Affect is sometimes employed as a quantitative term to express the person's emotional capacity and the degree of his reaction to given situations and sometimes rather loosely interchanged with other words which refer to either general or specific emotional conditions.

aggression: bold and energetic pursuit of one's ends; often used in the negative sense of expressing hostile and destructive action; sometimes interchanged with *aggressive drive* in the psychoanalytic literature.

aggressive drive: one of the two inherited urges (or instincts) hypothesized by Freud as providing the raw material of all mental life of human beings; frequently referred to as the *death instinct* (*Thanatos*) and thought to give rise to the destructive components of human behavior in contradistinction to the *sexual instinct* (*Eros*).

ambivalence: the bipolarity of feeling; that is, the tendency to be drawn in opposite emotional directions, as between love and hate, acceptance and rejection, denial and affirmation.

analytical psychology: the term applied to the deviant form of *psychoanalysis* developed by Carl Jung (see Section C of Chapter 4).

analytic group therapy: the theories and practices of *group therapy* of those who have a general psychoanalytic orientation (see Section B of Chapter 9).

anima: in Jungian analysis, the feminine component of the *psyche.*

animus: in Jungian analysis, the masculine component of the *psyche*.

anxiety: a feeling of a dreadful or fearsome threat, usually of such a vague nature that the person cannot correctly identify its specific source. In the Freudian literature, "*objective anxiety*" is the term used for apprehensiveness with a cause clearly identified in external reality. In Horneyian discussions, the term "*basic anxiety*" is employed to refer to the universal, childhood-derived feelings of loneliness and helplessness. Sullivan, on the other hand, generally employed the term *anxiety* to refer to a general, potent, restrictive force in the development of the individual, first "caught" by a process of contagion (which Sullivan called *empathy*) from the *mothering one* during infancy. *Anxiety,* in short, is a much used and variously defined word in the psychotherapeutic literature.

assertion-structured therapy: the term applied to the system of *psychotherapy* developed by E. Lakin Phillips (see Section D of Chapter 8).

behavior: while variously (and sometimes unclearly) used in psychological and physiological writings, the term is usually employed in the psychotherapeutic literature to refer to anything a human being does: that is, any act or succession of acts.

birth trauma: the damaging effect on the *psyche* of the transition from uterine to extrauterine environment. In the Rankian literature, the *birth trauma* is treated as the fundamental *anxiety* experience out of which most subsequent neurotic conditions of the individual grow.

catharsis: the release of tension and *anxiety* by recounting and/or *acting out* past experiences.

cathexis: in *psychoanalysis,* the amount of psychic energy which is directed toward or attached to the mental representative (that is, memories, thoughts, fantasies) of a person or thing. For example, *cathexis* is high in the *fantasy* a man has of his absent sweetheart (in this case much *libido* is channeled into his mental representation of his loved one; in other instances, *aggression* may be the chief form of psychic energy which is cathected).

character: sometimes used as a synonym of *personality,* but more often distinguished from the latter by its emphasis on volitional and moral aspects of human *behavior:* namely, the relatively consistent behavior tendencies of the individual in relation to moral issues and decisions affecting his relationships with others.

character armor: the term first employed by Wilhelm Reich for the system of *ego defenses* used by patients to resist the psychoanalytic probing of the sources of their *neuroses*. These resistances generally consist of such "good" *character* traits as obedience, co-operation, punctuality, and earnestness behind which the patient "hides" the traits which are likely to lead to the root of his troubles.

character neurosis: a type of psychic pathology or disorder relatively so stable and fixed that it seems an inseparable part of the individual's *personality*. Distinguished from a *psychoneurosis* (frequently referred to simply as a *neurosis*).

character structure: the sum and patterning of *character* traits; in Freudian theory, these traits are developed in the process of the *superego*'s efforts to control the *id*.

classical analysis (or *psychoanalysis*): used in two senses—(1) to distinguish the psychoanalytic theories and practices of the earlier Freudian period (with emphasis on unraveling the *unconscious* blockings of the *libido*) from those of the later Freudian period. In this sense, Chapter 2 treats *classical psychoanalysis,* and Chapter 3 deals with later Freudian developments. (2) The term is also sometimes employed to refer to the hypotheses and techniques of Freud and his followers as opposed to those of all psychoanalytic deviants. With this latter meaning, Chapters 2 and 3 may be considered *classical psychoanalysis*. (The first interpretation is the more common.)

client-centered therapy: the term applied to the system of *psychotherapy* developed by Carl Rogers (see Chapter 6).

collective unconscious: in Jungian theory, that part of the individual's *unconscious* which is hereditary and which the individual shares with other human beings. Sometimes called the *racial unconscious*.

compromise formation: (1) in Freudian dream interpretation, the consciously perceived (or manifest) dream, which represents an accommodation between the effort of a wish which has been repressed to seek fulfillment and the effort of the *ego* to defend itself against this disapproved impulse from the *id;* (2) in the Freudian theory of psychoneurosis, a similar adjustment between the incompletely repressed id impulse and the not fully effective *ego defenses* brings about a *psychosomatic symptom*.

compulsiveness: the tendency to repeat over and over inappropriate *behavior* and to be unable to keep from doing so (see *obsession* and *obsessive-compulsive reaction*).

conditioned reflex therapy: the term applied to the system of *psychotherapy* developed by Andrew Salter (see Section E of Chapter 7).

conditioning: the process whereby a form of behavior is elicited by a stimulus other than the originally effective (or natural or unconditioned) stimulus. The classical example (after Pavlov) is the dog which originally salivates with the presentation of food, has a bell rung with such presentation, and is soon conditioned to salivate upon hearing the bell alone. The term is sometimes used loosely to refer to all learning, but is seldom encountered in other psychotherapeutic writings than those referred to in Sections E and F of Chapter 7.

congruence: in the writings of Carl Rogers, the *personality* state in which the individual's actual *behavior* is in harmony with his self perceptions; the term is used to convey the notion of a *personality* which is genuine and integrated, as opposed to false and disturbed (see *incongruence*).

conscious: in *psychoanalysis,* a division of the *psyche* which includes those parts of mental life of which the person is at any moment aware; distinguished from the *preconscious* and the *unconscious.*

consensual validation: in the writings of Sullivan, the corrective experience for an individual's *parataxic distortions;* the process whereby a person reaches a more realistic point of view by comparing his thoughts and feelings with those of his associates.

death instinct: in the later writings of Freud, a basic drive of similar importance to the *sexual instinct;* also referred to as the *aggressive drive, aggression,* and *Thanatos.*

defense mechanism: any psychological instrumentality by which the individual protects his *ego* from *anxiety*-inducing *id* impulses; mechanisms commonly discussed in the Freudian literature include *repression, rationalization, projection, introjection, regression, turning against the self, isolation, thought dissociation, reaction formation,* and *denial of reality.* These mechanisms are also often termed *ego defenses.*

denial of reality: the *ego defense* which prevents admission to consciousness of external stimuli that point to the existence of feared *id* impulses.

depth-oriented therapy: any form of *psychotherapy* which professes to treat the *unconscious* sources of an individual's problems; often, more specifically, some form of *psychoanalysis.*

direct analysis: the term applied to the system of *psychotherapy* developed by John Rosen (see Section E of Chapter 5).

directive psychotherapy: the term applied to the system of psychotherapy developed by Frederick Thorne (see Section A of Chapter 8).

disowning: in the writings of Carl Rogers, the process whereby the individual avoids being aware of experiences and needs which have not been symbolized and which are inconsistent with the *self.* Roughly comparable to Freudian *repression* and Sullivanian *dissociation.*

displacement: in *psychoanalysis,* the substitution of one idea or image by another which is associatively connected with it.

dissociation: in Sullivanian theory, the process whereby the individual excludes from awareness those aspects of his experience which lead to acute *anxiety* (see *repression*—Freud, and *disowning*—Rogers).

distributive analysis and synthesis: the phrase applied to the characteristic procedures of *psychobiologic therapy.*

dynamic culturalists: the term applied to the psychoanalytic theories and practices of those who deviate from the teachings of Freud by placing less emphasis on the instinctive and more emphasis on the changing social sources of human *behavior* (see Sections A through D in Chapter 5).

dynamism: in Sullivanian theory, a relatively enduring configuration of energy found in interpersonal relations—sometimes applied to the whole *self* (self *dynamism*) and other times to patterns of energy organized around specific needs (lust *dynamism;* oral *dynamism*).

ego: in psychoanalysis, that part of the *psyche* which is the executant for the drives, the mediator between the *id* and the external environment.

ego defenses: see *defense mechanisms.*

Electra complex: in *psychoanalysis* (but rare other than in Jungian writings), the repressed desire of a female for incestuous relations with her father and for the destruction of her mother; the female version of the *Oedipus complex.*

empathy: (1) the acceptance and understanding of the feelings of another person, but with sufficient detachment to avoid becoming directly involved in those feelings; (2) in Sullivanian theory, a kind of vague, biologically derived process whereby the infant senses the emotions of the mothering one through "contagion and communion."

Eros: in psychoanalysis, the *sexual instinct* or *libido;* contrasted with *Thanatos,* the *death instinct.*

euphoria: an emotional attitude or feeling tone of health and vigor—"all is well."

excitation: the process whereby activity is set up in a nerve or in a muscle by nerve action; generalized in Salter's theory to refer to a state in the individual in which he is ready for vigorous action (opposed to *inhibition*).

existential analysis: the term applied to the system of *psychotherapy* which combines some of the teachings of existential philosophy with some of the theories and practices of *psychoanalysis* (see Section F of Chapter 5).

experiential therapy: the term applied to the system of *psychotherapy* developed by Carl Whitaker and Thomas Malone (see Section D of Chapter 7).

extroversion: an attitude of interest in things outside oneself rather than in one's own thoughts and feelings; opposite of *introversion.*

facial talk: a method used by Salter in his system of *conditioned-reflex therapy* to help a patient to overcome his *inhibitions* by learning to frankly show his emotions on his face.

family therapy: a type of *group therapy* undertaken with families (see Section D of Chapter 9).

fantasy: imagining a complex object or event (existent or non-existent) in concrete symbols or images, usually in the pleasant sense of a wish-fulfillment.

feeling-talk: a method used by Salter in his system of *conditioned-reflex therapy* to help a patient to overcome his *inhibitions* by saying what he (the patient) feels whenever he feels it.

free association: the chief therapeutic method developed by Freud—the patient is asked to begin with some remark or dream item and to state whatever comes to mind. The associative activity is (ideally) free of both the suggestions of the analyst and the *suppressions* of the patient.

genital maturity: in Freudian psychoanalysis, the goal toward which the developing *libido* is striving; distinguished from the *pregenital stages.*

Gestalt: a German word with approximate English equivalents of configuration, meaningful organized whole, structural relationship, and theme.

Gestalt therapy: the term applied to the system of *psychotherapy* developed by Frederick Perls, Ralph F. Hefferline, and Paul Goodman (see Section B of Chapter 7).

group-centered therapy: the term applied to the system of *group therapy* developed by Carl Rogers and associates (see Section C of Chapter 9).

group therapy: any form of *psychotherapy* in which several persons are treated simultaneously (see Chapter 9).

hostility: tendency to feel anger toward and to seek to inflict harm upon a person or group.

hypnoanalysis: psychoanalysis carried on while the patient is under *hypnosis.*

hypnosis: a state characterized by greatly heightened suggestibility, usually attained by bodily relaxation accompanied by concentration on a narrow range of stimuli presented by the hypnotist.

hypnotherapy: psychotherapy which utilizes techniques of *hypnosis* (see Section C of Chapter 7).

hysteria: a kind of catch-all form of *neurosis* in which patients manifest such variable sensory, motor, vasomotor, visceral, and mental symptoms as paralyzed limbs, deafness, blindness, and other pathological conditions for which no anatomical or physiological causes could be found. Such patients were much more numerous in the latter part of the 19th and early part of the 20th centuries than currently. The term is not included in the most recent standard psychiatric nomenclature.

id: in *psychoanalysis,* that part of the *psyche* from which the instinctive impulses (namely, the *sexual instinct* and the *death instinct*) emerge; the *id* contains the blind, impersonal, primary emotions from which all behavior springs. Part of the *id's* energy is utilized to form the other aspects of the *psyche* (the *ego* and *superego*).

idealized self image: in Horneyian theory, a pattern of perfectionistic strivings and godlike fantasies which constitute the core of a *neurosis.*

id level therapy: any method of *psychotherapy* which proposes to reach the deeper levels of the *unconscious.* Less common as a term than *depth-oriented therapy.*

identification: (1) the process of becoming like something or someone in one or several aspects of behavior; (2) in *psychoanalysis,* as a *defense mechanism, identification* is sometimes used interchangeably with *introjection.*

incongruence: in the writings of Carl Rogers, the *personality* state in which the individual's actual *behavior* and experience is in disharmony with his *self* perceptions. When the individual is aware of such disharmony, he is anxious; when he is unaware, he is vulnerable to *anxiety.*

individual psychology: the term applied to the system of *psychotherapy* developed by Alfred Adler (see Section A of Chapter 4).

inhibition: stopping a process from continuing, or preventing a process from starting, even though the usual stimulus which elicits the process is present; generalized in Salter's *conditioned-reflex therapy* to refer to any restraint in the range, amount, and effectiveness of behavior (opposed to *excitation*).

insight: the process by which the meaning, significance, pattern, or use of an experience becomes clear—or the understanding which results from this process.

instinct: an unlearned and enduring tendency to act in an organized way that is characteristic of a given species; in his later writings, Freud recognized two irreducible instincts: *Eros* (the *sexual instinct*) and *Thanatos* (the *death instinct*).

interference theory: the hypotheses on which *assertion-structured therapy* is based.

interpersonal relations: the interactions between two or more persons, or the characteristic pattern of such interactions; the reciprocal involvements of two or more people. Most commonly employed in Sullivan's writings.

introjection: a *defense mechanism;* the *ego* protects itself against an impulse from the *id* that is *anxiety*-producing by taking in (that is, identifying itself with) another person. The opposite of *projection.*

introversion: an attitude of interest in one's own thoughts and feelings rather than external events; opposite of *extroversion.*

isolation: in *psychoanalysis,* (1) *thought dissociation;* (2) the *defense mechanism* whereby the *affect* connected with a painful past event is repressed.

juvenile era: in Sullivan's writings, the stage in a child's development which begins when he shows a need for playmates and lasts until the emergence of a need for an intimate relationship with another person of comparable status at *preadolescence*.

learning: all the processes by means of which an individual is changed so that at a later time his actions or reactions are not what they would have been without the previous activity.

learning theory: an attempt to state the general nature of *learning*.

learning theory therapy: the term applied to a system of *psychotherapy* developed by several psychologists (see Section C of Chapter 8).

libido: (1) in Freudian *psychoanalysis,* the *sexual instinct, Eros;* (2) in Jungian (and, confusedly, some Freudian) writings, a life force or instinct which has been somehow vaguely desexualized.

life plan: life style.

life style: in Adler's writings, an individual's characteristic and pervasive pattern of *behavior* for dealing with his feelings of inferiority and for gaining status.

manic-depressive psychosis: a *psychosis* of marked emotional oscillation.

masochism: in *psychoanalysis,* the turning of any sort of destructive tendencies inward upon oneself.

mothering one: the term used by Sullivan to refer to the person (mother or mother substitute) who most significantly influences the individual during infancy.

multiple therapy: any form of *psychotherapy* in which two or more therapists simultaneously participate.

need: a tension induced in the individual by the lack of something which, if present, would tend to further his welfare.

neo-Freudian analysis: the psychoanalytic theories and practices of *therapists* who claim to have revised, rather than to have rejected, the teachings of Freud. In practical effect, all psychoanalysts (except Adler, Stekel, Jung, Rank, and their followers) are either Freudian or *neo-Freudian:* the former if they make no major deviations from Freudian hypotheses or procedures and the latter if they do. Some "Freudian loyalists," however, at times seem more revisionist than neo-Freudians.

neurasthenia: a *psychoneurosis* characterized by feelings of weakness and the general lowering of bodily and mental tone; no longer included in the standard psychiatric nomenclature.

neurosis: psychoneurosis. While Freud made a distinction between what he called actual neuroses and psychoneuroses in his early writings, he and his followers later dropped the distinction.

neurotic need: in Horney's writings, a strategy employed by an anxious person to find a solution to the problems of disturbed human relationships and to cope with his feelings of isolation and helplessness; it takes the form of a compulsive demand for certain behavior on the part of others.

nondirective therapy: client-centered therapy.

objective psychotherapy: the term applied to the system of *psychotherapy* developed by Benjamin Karpman (see Section E of Chapter 5).

obsession: an idea, usually associated with anxiety, that persists or frequently recurs and cannot be dismissed by the individual.

obsessive-compulsive reaction: a type of *psychoneurosis* in which *anxiety* is associated with *obsessions* and compulsions (see *compulsiveness*).

Oedipus complex: feelings of rivalry and hostility toward one parent and of incestuous desire for the other parent. Originally the *Oedipus complex* was used by Freud to refer to the desire of the boy for his mother in hostile competition with his father, but the term has been extended to include comparable behavior in the girl (see *Electra complex*). The situation is also sometimes reversed: the child shows sexual desire for the parent of the same sex and jealousy and murderous rage toward the parent of the other sex (termed an inverted Oedipus).

orgone therapy: a term applied to a system of physical therapy developed by Wilhelm Reich. Also called *vegetotherapy.*

paranoid tendency: evidence of grandiose ideas and/or sensitivity to real or apparent criticism. The delusions of persecution and grandiosity may appear in a rare form of *psychosis* called paranoia, in paranoid *schizophrenia,* or in a sufficiently mild and peripheral and socially insignificant form as to be diagnosed as *psychoneurosis* (or even eccentricity).

parapraxis: a minor error in behavior, such as a slip of the tongue or pen, memory blockings, small accidents, misplacing articles, etc. In *psychoanalysis,* a *parapraxis* is never considered accidental, always caused by some *unconscious* conflict. Popularly called "a Freudian slip."

parataxic distortion: a reaction, in *interpersonal relations,* to a *personification* rather than (or in addition to) an actual person; that is, any attitude toward another person based on *fantasy* or on *identification* of that person with other figures. This is a Sullivanian term which includes the phenomena the Freudians call *transference* and many additional forms of *displacement* and *projection.*

persona: in Jungian writings, the mask of conscious intentions and fulfillments of social requirements of the individual behind which he hides (from himself as well as others) his more deeply rooted components of *personality;* the role which a person plays.

personality: (1) all the mental or *behavior* traits of a person, the sum total of psychological traits; the individual's integrated system of traits or *behavior* tendencies; (2) those aspects of the individual's nature which have developed in social relationships and have other persons or social values as their object. Definition (1) more broadly includes all psychological characteristics of the individual, whether or not derived from or relevant to *interpersonal relations*. These two meanings (and many more) are found confusedly interchanged in the literature.

personification: a type of *projection* in which an individual attributes favorable or unfavorable qualities to another person as a result of his own *unconscious* conflicts.

phenomenal field: everything, including awareness of the *self,* experienced by an individual at any moment. Objects physically present, but not perceived, are not part of the *phenomenal field,* and objects not physically present, but thought about, are.

phenomenological point of view: the hypothesis that an individual's *behavior* may be entirely understood and explained in terms of his *phenomenal field;* particularly applicable to the theoretical formulations of *client-centered therapy* and *existential analysis.*

phobia: a morbid, persistent, excessive fear of some particular type of object or situation; the source of the fear is at least partly irrational and *unconscious.* The term has recently become rare in the literature, and the former tendency to compound the word with others of Greek origin (as in acrophobia, agoraphobia, claustrophobia—fear, respectively, of high, open, and closed places) is now even rarer.

pleasure principle: in psychoanalysis, the demand of the *id* for immediate gratification of an *instinct* (see *primary process*). In infancy, the individual is dominated by the *pleasure principle,* but as the *ego* develops, he becomes aware of the demands of reality (see *reality principle*).

preadolescence: in Sullivanian analysis, the chum period in the development of the individual, which follows upon the *juvenile era* and ends with the eruption of genital sexuality and a change of strong interest from a person of one's own sex to a person of the other sex.

preconscious: in psychoanalysis, a division of the *psyche* which includes those parts of mental life which have ready access to consciousness. Any thought which happens to be *conscious* at a given moment is *preconscious* both before and after that particular moment. Compare with *unconscious.*

pregenital stages: see *stages of sexuality.*

primary process: the characteristic functioning of the *id,* whereby there is immediate and direct satisfaction of an *instinct.* The *id,* according to Freud, does not discriminate between fantasy and reality; hence, if an instinct fails to obtain discharge through a motor exit, it will take an unconscious *sensory* route (notably through dreams in healthy individuals and through hallucination in the mentally ill) via the remembered perception of a previous satisfaction. *Primary process* thinking is the dominant mode for the young child and persists in the *unconscious* in adult life and manifests itself chiefly through dreams, humor, pathology (see *secondary process*).

projection: (1) the process of attributing one's own traits, problems, or points of view to others; (2) used as a *defense mechanism,* the individual protects his *ego* from the recognition of an undesirable *id* impulse by relocating the impulse in another person.

psyche: (1) roughly, the mind (or organized totality of all mental processes or psychological activities); (2) the aspect of the human being which performs psychological functions. Some writers use *psyche* and mind interchangeably; some avoid one term or the other; and some make rather unclear distinctions between the two along the lines of meanings (1) and (2).

psychic determinism: the postulate that psychic or mental processes are never fortuitous, but are completely explainable in terms of their causes.

psychoanalysis: (1) the term applied to the system of *psychotherapy* developed by Sigmund Freud (see Chapters 2 and 3); (2) any system of *psychotherapy* so designated either by its proponents or others. Although Karen Horney, for example (see Section A of Chapter 5), gradually developed a system that departed so markedly from Freud's teachings that she was disowned and denounced by many other psychoanalysts, she continued to consider her theories revisionist and, hence, *neo-Freudian analysis.* Alfred Adler, on the other hand, engaged in a process of reciprocal disowning with Freud and developed his system of *individual psychology,* which both he and Freud considered something other than *psychoanalysis.* Still, by popular usage, Adler's system is (at least in the United States) considered a form of *psychoanalysis.*

psychobiologic therapy: the term applied to the system of *psychotherapy* developed by Adolf Meyer (see Section A of Chapter 7).

psychodrama: the improvised enactment by a client of certain roles and incidents, prescribed by the therapist or spontaneously originating in the client. This therapeutic *acting out* is designed to reveal underlying causes of irrational *behavior* and is usually a part of *group therapy* (see Section A of Chapter 9).

psychometric test: any device designed to obtain a quantitative assessment of an individual's psychological attributes.

psychoneurosis: a disorder of *behavior* characterized by *anxiety,* which may be directly experienced or controlled by *defense mechanisms,* in which there is no gross disorganization of *personality* or great distortion of reality perception, and for which *psychotherapy* is often indicated. The disorder is now quite commonly designated as *neurosis;* it should be distinguished from *character neurosis* and *psychosis.*

psychosis: a disorder of *behavior* in which there is considerable disorganization of *personality* and readily recognizable distortion of reality perception and for which medical treatment (and sometimes hospitalization) in addition to *psychotherapy* is often indicated. The chief so-called "functional psychoses" (where no specific organic causes have been established) are *manic-depressive psychosis* and *schizophrenia.* The distinction between *psychosis* and a severe form of *psychoneurosis* is frequently less than clear in a clinical setting.

psychosomatic symptom: a sign of a bodily malfunctioning which is believed to have originated from, or to have been aggravated by, a psychological malfunctioning. Hives, for example, are thought to derive, at times, from a feeling of resentment.

psychotherapy: the use of any psychological technique in the treatment of mental disorder or social and emotional maladjustment.

psychotherapy by reciprocal inhibition: the term applied to the system of *psychotherapy* developed by Joseph Wolpe (see Section F of Chapter 7).

rapport: a reciprocally comfortable and unconstrained relationship between two or more persons, especially between therapist and patient.

rationalization: (1) the process of concocting plausible reasons to account for one's practices or beliefs which actually derive from other sources; (2) a *defense mechanism* in which the *ego* changes the nature of a thought or feeling (which is associated with a repressed *id* impulse) in order to make it more acceptable. Meaning (2) differs from meaning (1) mainly in its use of psychoanalytic terms related to causation.

rational psychotherapy: the term applied to the system of *psychotherapy* developed by Albert Ellis (see Section E of Chapter 8).

reaction formation: a *defense mechanism* (used in situations where *ambivalence* exists) in which the *ego* protects itself from aggressive *id* impulses by the *conscious* emphasis of positive feelings, such as love, protection, and tenderness.

reaction type: a psychiatric diagnostic classification in terms of the preponderating symptom; historically associated with *psychobiologic therapy.*

reality principle: the process by which the *ego* becomes aware of the demands of the environment and works out an adjustment between these demands and the basic *needs* of the *id*. The *reality principle* utilizes the *secondary process.*

reconnaissance: that part of *therapy* characterized by the collection of biographical information about the patient through intensive interrogation (Sullivan).

reconstructive therapy: any *psychotherapy* which professes to effect major changes in the *personality* of a patient. Often associated with *depth-level therapy* and contrasted with *re-educative therapy.*

redundancy: in *assertion-structured therapy,* circular and self-defeating behavior, developed as a result of the individual's persisting in assertions which meet with disconfirmation. The stronger the assertions, the greater the *redundancy*.

re-educative therapy: any system of *psychotherapy* which is believed to help the individual to handle his problems more effectively rather than to reconstruct his *personality*. Contrasted with *reconstructive therapy*. In general, proponents of a system are likely to claim that it is *reconstructive,* opponents are apt to label it "merely" *re-educative*.

regression: in *psychoanalysis,* (1) the process in which the individual, under the influence of emotional strain, returns to *behavior* characteristic of an earlier *stage of genitality;* (2) as a *defense mechanism,* essentially the same process is utilized in a more transitory way as a means of protecting the *ego* from being overwhelmed by *id* impulses.

reinforcement: any circumstance or event that increases the probability that a response will recur in a situation like that in which the reinforcing condition originally occurred; or, quite generally, any condition strengthening *learning*.

repression: the first recognized and most basic of the *defense mechanisms;* the *unconscious* activity of the ego which keeps the undesirable *id* impulse (or any feeling, wish, memory, or *fantasy* associated with it) from entering consciousness.

resistance: in *psychoanalysis,* opposition to any attempt to get at the unconscious; more generally, opposition offered by a patient to the orders, actions, recommendations, or suggestions of the therapist.

sadism: the compulsive tendency to vent *aggression* and destructiveness on another person; overt sexual satisfaction may or may not accompany this *behavior*.

satisfaction: in Sullivanian terminology, the fulfillment of a basic biological *need,* including sleep and rest, sex fulfillment, food and drink, and physical closeness to other human animals. Distinguished from *security*.

schizophrenia: a group of *psychoses* characterized by major disturbances in reality relationships, by blurring of thought processes by fantasy and personal desires, and by marked behavioral disturbances (often with progressive deterioration of the *personality*). Many types of schizophrenia are distinguished clinically, of which simple, paranoid, hebephrenic, and catatonic forms are most common.

secondary process: the characteristic functioning of the *ego* in which it fulfills *id* impulses by indirect routes (contrast with *primary process*) while at the same time meeting the demands of the external environment (see *reality principle*).

sector therapy: the term applied to the system of *psychotherapy* developed by Felix Deutsch (see Section E of Chapter 5).

security: in Sullivanian terminology, a state of *euphoria,* of belonging, of being accepted. Distinguished from *satisfaction.*

selective inattention: not being guided in behavior by an aspect of the situation that is perceived.

self: (1) that aspect of the person which carries out psychological, as distinguished from physiological, activities; (2) the individual revealed to his own observation as the identical and persistent center of psychological processes (Rogers); (3) that part of the personality which has alertness, which notices what goes on (Sullivan); (4) *actual self*—the total psychophysical being at a given moment, including both *conscious* and *unconscious* mechanisms (Horney); (5) *idealized self*—the perfected and glorified person which the neurotic believes himself to be after he unconsciously identifies with his previously imagined *idealized self-image* (Horney); (6) *real self*—the source of the energy that, in each individual, can be mobilized in the direction of constructive and healthy growth (Horney); (7) *true self*—all the potentialities of the individual which might be developed in the most favorable social milieu (Fromm).

self-concept: a person's view of himself; the fullest description of himself that a person is capable of giving at any particular time. This is similar to, if not identical with, meaning (2) of *self.*

self-dynamism: the pattern of the enduring motivations toward *satisfaction* and toward *security* that form the *self-system* (Sullivan).

self-system: the more or less final choice of potentialities that the individual seeks to develop and to integrate as a result of his formative experiences in *interpersonal relations* (Sullivan).

semantics: (1) the science of meanings of words or other signs; (2) *general semantics*—the term applied to a system of *psychotherapy* based on applied *semantics* (see Section B of Chapter 8).

sexual instinct: in *psychoanalysis,* an inconsistently employed term for pleasure-seeking and life-expressing *id* impulses and *unconscious* drives. Originally Freud used *sexual instinct* (and the synonym *libido*) to refer directly or indirectly to sexual craving or erotic desire, but, in his later writings, seemed to veer toward the less specifically erotic meanings of general pleasure-seeking and life-expressing (*Eros*).

socialization: the processes by which an individual acquires sensitivity to the demands of group life and learns to get along with and to behave similarly to other members of the group.

stages of development: (1) *stages of sexuality;* (2) in Sullivanian theory, the periods in the individual's development characteristically related to various patterns of *interpersonal relations* (infancy, childhood, *juvenile era, preadolescence,* early adolescence, late adolescence, and adulthood).

stages of sexuality: in Freudian theory, the developmental periods through which the individual is pushed by the *libido* toward the achievement of mature sexuality. The first period, characteristic of the first year of life, is the oral stage, during which the libidinal energy is centered in the mouth. The second is the anal stage, usually extending from age 1 through age 3, during which the *libido* is partially transferred to the anal zone. In this phase the child derives great pleasures from the retention and expulsion of feces. The third period is the phallic stage, during which interest is first focused on the penis (or clitoris), but soon fastens upon the parents. This third phase is sometimes referred to as the Oedipus period (see *Oedipus complex*). All three stages are called *pregenital stages* to distinguish them from the normal adult state, *genital maturity*.

structural hypothesis, the third and last theory of the *psyche* proposed by Freud, in which he distinguished three functionally related structures of the *psyche:* the *id,* the *ego,* and the *superego.* Distinguished from the *topographic theory.*

sublimation: in Freudian theory, the alteration of the channels of the *libido* in such a way as to bring the expression of the *sexual instinct* within the bonds of conventional approval. For example, the infantile wish to play with feces (expression of the *libido* at the *anal stage*) may be sublimated by playing with mud (and, still later in life, by sculpturing in clay).

superego: in *psychoanalysis,* that part of the *psyche* which comprises the individual's moral precepts and ideal aspirations; it is mainly developed in the Oedipal period and is largely an internalization of parental standards as perceived by the *ego.*

suppression: in *psychoanalysis,* a *conscious* exclusion of disapproved desires; contrasted with *repression,* in which the process of exclusion is not conscious.

Thanatos: the *death instinct.*

therapist: one who conducts treatment procedures; the agent who provides *psychotherapy.*

therapy: psychotherapy.

thought dissociation: a *defense mechanism* by which the *ego* protects itself from a thought that carries with it dangerous *id* impulses—the ego dissociates this thought from thoughts that preceded it and thoughts which follow it. The individual experiences momentary mental blankness; sometimes called *isolation.*

topographic theory: Freud's effort to develop a map of the *psyche* by dividing its contents and operations into three mental systems: Ucs. (*unconscious*), Pcs. (*preconscious*), and Cs. (*conscious*). This was the second of three theories of the psyche formulated by Freud. The first was an unnamed hypothesis which compared the mind to an optical instrument; the third was the *structural hypothesis*.

transference: in *psychoanalysis,* the *displacement* of *affect* from one object to another; specifically, the process whereby a patient shifts feelings applicable to another person (often a parent) onto the psychoanalyst.

trauma: damage or injury to the *psyche;* an experience or set of experiences (plural, traumas or traumata) that inflicts serious injury.

turning against the self: a *defense mechanism* whereby the *ego* (usually of a child) protects itself from a forbidden *aggressive* impulse against another person which it (the *ego*) dare not consciously admit by self-berating or self punishment. The child is, in effect, temporarily being the hated person (often a parent) and thus striking or berating that person by striking or berating himself.

unconscious: in *psychoanalysis,* a division of the *psyche* the contents of which are at least temporarily (and usually permanently) unknown to the individual. This part of the *psyche,* Freud hypothesized, contains the mental processes which are of fundamental significance and frequency in human *behavior* and are usually the causes of human actions. Also see *collective unconscious.*

value: (1) an abstract concept, often merely implicit, that defines what ends or means to an end are desirable; (2) a goal; (3) the degree of worth ascribed to an object or activity.

vegetotherapy: orgone therapy.

will therapy: the term applied to the system of *psychotherapy* developed by Otto Rank (see Section D of Chapter 4).

Index

R